THE
FEDERAL ROLE
IN
LIBRARY
AND
INFORMATION
SERVICES

by Marilyn Gell Mason

Knowledge Industry Publications, Inc.
White Plains, NY and London

Professional Librarian Series

The Federal Role in Library and Information Services

Library of Congress Cataloging in Publication Data

Mason, Marilyn Gell.
　　The federal role in library and information services.

　　(Professional librarian series)
　　Bibliography: p.
　　Includes index.
　　1. Libraries and state--United States. 2. Information
services and state--United States. 3. Government informa-
tion--United States.　I. Title.　II. Series.
Z678.2.M37　1983　　025.5′2′0973　　83-11970
ISBN 0-86729-010-2
ISBN 0-86729-009-9 (pbk.)

Printed in the United States of America

10　9　8　7　6　5　4　3　2　1

Table of Contents

List of Tables and Figures

To Bob and Charlie

1

Introduction

Many members of the library community see the federal role in library and information services almost exclusively as that of a funding source. To be sure, since 1956, when the Library Services Act was passed, federal grants-in-aid programs have played an important and highly visible role in library development.

But federal involvement in library services actually began almost 200 years ago, when Congress enacted a bill creating the Library of Congress. Federal involvement in shaping information policy began at an even earlier date, when our founding fathers included the First Amendment in the Constitution and authorized the establishment of "post offices and post roads." From these embryonic beginnings, the federal role in library and information services has grown to what it is today: multitiered and multifaceted, reflecting both the changing responsibilities of government and the evolving needs of an increasingly technological society.

This book examines the past, present and future roles of the federal government in nationwide library development. In doing so, it finds that federal involvement in support of library and information services is consistent with federal activity in other areas, and that the same political, economic and technological principles that shape library-related programs are also at work shaping other parts of our social structure. As a result, any complete analysis of federal roles in library and information services must be set in a broader context.

THE FEDERAL ROLES

Generally speaking, there are four roles that the federal government has played, does play and will continue to play in library development. They are:

- Data collection and distribution;
- Financial support through grants-in-aid;
- Research and demonstration; and
- Planning and policy making.

1

The following chapters describe the current level of federal activity in these areas. They assess the issues involved in each area, and examine options for future federal involvement. In addition, the chapters discuss several specific topics and events that provide examples of the influence and impact the federal government has had on library and information services.

POLITICS, ECONOMICS AND TECHNOLOGY

Library and information services are part of the society in which they exist. Thus, the same political, economic and technological forces that shape society also influence library services and the federal role in library development. Chapter 2 examines several of these underlying forces: political principles, economic conditions and principles, and technological change.

As Chapter 2 indicates, contemporary political philosophies hinge on the balance of three elements or ''tensions'' that have been part of our government since the founding of the nation: individual freedom versus the general welfare, sovereignty of states versus sovereignty of the federal government, and public sector versus private sector interests. Various balances between these values have been struck at different times in our history, and these balances have been reflected in the role assumed by the federal government in its library and information-related activities.

Economic conditions and principles have also helped to create the environment in which libraries exist. In spite of differences of opinion about how the economy can best be managed, there is some agreement about basic economic principles and concepts. Since any type of federal involvement in the development of library and information services requires an allocation of scarce financial resources, an understanding of these conditions and principles is essential to an evaluation of the federal responsibility.

Technological change has become a driving force in our society. Like the internal combustion engine of an earlier era, information technologies are shaping and changing all of our institutions. Because communications and computer technologies are specifically related to the mission of libraries, and because they are changing the capabilities of libraries and of the federal government itself, a description of these developments and a brief analysis of their potential is also included in Chapter 2.

The discussion of these three elements—political principles, economic conditions and principles, and technological change—provides the background necessary to understand why libraries and information centers have developed as they have and how they are likely to develop in the future. This conceptual framework also provides a mechanism for identifying the most critical issues of the day, and for analyzing federal roles in the development of library and information services.

DATA COLLECTION AND DISTRIBUTION

The first of the federal roles both historically and in order of importance is the role the government plays in data collection and distribution. Since the earliest days of the republic, the federal government has recognized its responsibility to provide elected and appointed officials with the resources necessary to make informed decisions. As a result, it now spends over $15 billion per year on the production, publication, storage, distribution and use of scientific and technical information alone. Of that sum, over $500 million is spent on the operation of the three national libraries and the network of more than 2000 federal libraries.

Chapter 3 describes the activities of the federal government as both a consumer and distributor of information. Although the government's role in information *collection* is unquestioned, federal involvement in information *distribution* has been hotly debated of late. In this context, and with an eye toward the principles established in Chapter 2, the federal role as information distributor is examined. The discussion includes an analysis of the activities of the Joint Committee on Printing, the Government Printing Office, the Depository Library Program and the National Technical Information Service.

GRANTS-IN-AID

Federal grants-in-aid programs are a smaller and less stable investment that the federal government makes in nationwide library development. Together, federal aid programs to public libraries, school libraries and libraries in institutions of higher education amount to approximately $250 million per year, or less than half the amount used to operate federal libraries alone. Moreover, these aid programs have been systematically attacked.

Chapter 4 describes the complete range of library aid programs, including funds for public libraries, school libraries, academic libraries, research libraries and medical libraries. It also examines the considerable impact that these programs have had on library development, despite the meagerness of the funds involved.

RESEARCH AND DEMONSTRATION

The federal government provides financial support for about one half of all research conducted in the United States. It also spends tens of billions of dollars on information processing. Nevertheless, the federal investment in library-related research and development is shockingly low. Chapter 5 examines the responsibility of the federal government to provide support for research and demonstration efforts in information areas.

If the U.S. hopes to continue its leading role in the new information economy, the nation must continue to develop its ability to collect and distribute information in an efficient and effective manner. This development depends on a solid investment in basic and applied research. In addition to documenting the federal role in general research and development, Chapter 5 also describes the specific R&D activities and contributions of the Department of Education's Library Programs Division and the National Institute of Education, the National Science Foundation, the National Endowment for the Humanities and others.

PLANNING AND POLICY MAKING

Information policy is a slippery and illusive term, and federal planning and policy making is often misunderstood. Chapter 6 examines the federal role in library planning and the establishment of national information policies. It describes the range of federal information policies, the planning activities of the Department of Education and the National Commission on Libraries and Information Science, and the impact of information policies on library planning and action. It also describes the policy-making activities of the courts, the Congress, the Office of Management and Budget, the Copyright Office of the Library of Congress and other executive departments.

In addition, Chapter 5 discusses several significant pieces of relevant legislation (the Freedom of Information Act, the Privacy Act of 1974 and the Paperwork Reduction Act of 1980) and several Office of Management and Budget regulatory documents. Finally, the chapter reexamines several of the issues identified in Chapter 2 from the perspective of current policy-making activities.

LIBRARY NETWORKS

Chapter 7 presents nationwide library networking as an example of how political, economic and technological conditions have combined to shape the federal role in the development of a specific type of service. Because library networking is a relatively recent phenomenon with a short and clearly visible history, it provides a particularly useful example of the interrelationship between the various federal roles in supporting and shaping library development. Moreover, economic conditions and technological change have themselves played major, clearly apparent roles in generating both the need for networks and the capability to establish networks.

WHITE HOUSE CONFERENCE

The 1979 White House Conference on Library and Information Services was probably the single largest, most political event dealing with libraries that has taken place in this country. As such, it has special significance. Chapter 8 examines the history of the Conference, its design and structure, and the issues discussed. It also looks at outcomes and assesses the degree to which the Conference achieved its goals.

While the White House Conference was an example of the federal government exercising its role as planner, it may be more important as an illustration of some of the political issues developed in Chapter 2. Conference participants were concerned about political principles, economic conditions and principles, and technological change. Moreover, the conference was a major attempt to look to the future in an effort to define the federal responsibility in a way that is consistent with the emerging library and information environment.

FUTURE FEDERAL ROLE

Chapter 9 gathers together the issues that have been identified in the course of this book. It reevaluates the rationale for federal involvement in light of recent trends, synthesizes emerging issues and explores potential developments.

In the future, library-related roles for the federal government will be to some extent a continuation of past activities modified by present needs and available resources. Thus, we can expect the federal government to continue to collect the data needed to operate the government itself and to distribute government-produced information in some manner. The diffusion of knowledge gained from these efforts will surely affect nationwide library development in significant ways.

Future federal roles will also rest on our understanding of the political process and our skill and will in using it. Thus, the continuation of grants-in-aid programs will largely depend on the degree to which the library profession is able to convince legislators that support for libraries is in their political best interests.

Research and demonstration activities as they relate to library and information services are likely to result from emerging economic and technological trends. In the coming years, as information technology becomes increasingly important in industry and business, we can expect the government to invest more research and development funding in technology areas. This investment will also benefit libraries, since individual libraries can often learn from research that is only tangentially related to their specific activities.

Planning and policy making is the most volatile area in which the federal government operates. It is also the area most closely tied to political philosophy. The federal government will certainly continue to establish policy at some level, but for libraries this policy making is most likely to flow from the various funding, research and development activities enumerated above. In general, we can expect a more decentralized approach to planning, at least in theory.

The American democracy depends on an informed public, and on the tension and balance between various levels and branches of government. Current political, economic and technological trends indicate that some reasonable objectives for future federal participation in library development are to:

• Support national libraries and federal libraries as important national resources;

• Encourage the expansion of state and local resources by providing financial incentives for library development;

• Encourage the continued growth of major research libraries by subsidizing resource development;

• Support research and development at an elevated level to achieve economies of scale, increased productivity and advances in information technology that might have spill-over effects on other parts of the economy;

• Promote use of the latest technology within the government itself, so that federal agencies become a model for information handling and spin-off systems, much as the Library of Congress has been;

• Provide a mechanism for the establishment and promulgation of standards;

• Adopt a laissez-faire approach to the development of bibliographic utilities and state and regional networks, with the exception of support for research and development;

• Maintain an aggressive approach to federal information distribution; and

• Limit centralized library planning and policy making.

MAINTAINING THE BALANCE

The objectives above are consistent with current political trends, economic imperatives and technological capabilities. In addition, they suggest that the federal government should not try to provide everything needed for nationwide library development. Democracy is often a messy process. The efficiency fallacy might lead us to expect the federal government to provide central direction and massive financial support. But the goal of a democratic form of government is not efficiency but balance, and with balance comes tension.

Tension, balance and occasional discomfort have brought us to where we are. Patterns of library development vary, and this variety has brought richness and growth to agencies charged with providing access to information. The responsibility of the federal government is to build on strength, encourage diversity and maintain balance among many competing interests.

Information is indeed basic to our democratic form of government, and libraries are charged with providing public access to that information. Because unbiased information is of such importance, libraries must be especially sensitive to the need to remain balanced and objective.

In the future, the library's mission is likely to become even more difficult and complex. For example, while libraries must continue to fight for government funding and support, they must also continue to play a key role in maintaining the balance between individual and societal interests, between various levels and branches of government, and between public and private groups. In the final analysis, the degree to which libraries come to compete and cooperate with America's growing private information companies is likely to prove particularly important.

2

Why Federal Involvement?

The history of federal involvement in library development closely parallels the growth of the federal government itself and the changing nature and role of libraries in American society. The first direct action taken by the U.S. Congress in support of libraries occurred in 1800, when the Library of Congress was established to meet the needs of the new legislature. In 1836 the federal government founded the Library of the Surgeon General's Office. This later grew into what is now the National Library of Medicine. Today, the federal government maintains numerous libraries and information centers to support its own activities, provides grants-in-aid for nationwide library development, takes part in needed research and development, and enacts legislation and regulations that establish the parameters of information policy.

This chapter will examine three forces that shape the environment in which library and information services are developed and distributed: political principles, economic conditions and principles, and technological change. Libraries do not exist in a vacuum. They are part of a dynamic and continually changing social structure. Political, economic and technological shifts establish the broader role of the federal government, and it is out of this broader definition of federal roles that the impact of the federal government on library and information services can be most clearly seen.

POLITICAL PRINCIPLES

Democracy as practiced in the United States rests on tension and ambiguity. Tension flows from the structural division of power both within the federal government and between the federal government and state governments, and ambiguity characterizes the language used in the documents that created the government. Tension and ambiguity also run through the principles that motivated the establishment of our form of government and that continue to shape its values.

The primary values articulated during the founding of the nation and repeatedly throughout its history are individual rights, states' rights and property rights. These values may also be described as conflicts among three sets of competing values: 1) the freedom of the individual versus the good of the people as a whole; 2) sovereignty of the states versus the sovereignty of the federal government; and 3) private sector economic interests versus public sector responsibilities.

Each of these values contains tension and ambiguity. Throughout our history, the tension has allowed us to maintain balance among competing interests, while the ambiguity has allowed us to interpret the principles in a manner that is appropriate to a particular time. As a matter of policy, the United States has tried to protect the interests of both the individual and society, the states and the federal government, and the public and the private sectors. It is a matter of balance. Of course, at times in our history, the balance has tilted more toward one side or the other in each of these pairings, but the tension remains, and out of that tension comes growth. Organisms, whether biological or political, atrophy when their capacities go untested.

Each of these areas also represents one aspect of federal responsibility. The federal government may be seen as a defender of individual freedoms or a protector of the general welfare. It may be perceived as a union of states or as a governmental unit apart from the states. It may be considered a promoter of private enterprise or a corporate competitor. Given a changing set of circumstances, any or all of these descriptions may be more or less true at a given time.

Individual Rights

Some historians feel that our founding fathers were "interested less in the ideology— the formulation of a systematic philosophy—than in the technology of politics."[1] That is to say that Jefferson, Madison, Hamilton and the rest were pragmatists. They were concerned with creating a government that would both work in the present and adapt to the future. They were confident if not entirely comfortable with the notion that "We may safely trust to the wisdom of our successors the remedies of evils to arise."[2]

If there was an ideology, it flowed from a confidence in human reason. John Stuart Mill captured this basic belief in describing his father:

> So complete was my father's reliance on the influence of reason over the
> minds of mankind, whenever it was allowed to reach them, that he felt that
> all would be gained if the whole population were taught to read, if all sorts
> of opinions were allowed to be addressed to them by work and writing, and
> if by means of the suffrage they could nominate a legislature to give effect to
> the opinions they adopted.[3]

This generally optimistic view of human nature found its way into a form of government concerned above all with the "inalienable rights" of its citizens. Among those rights are certain freedoms, the most basic of which are freedom from oppression of any type by the government and freedom to participate in the government by voting for elected representatives. Commenting on the sovereignty of the American people, Alexis de Tocqueville observed: "The people reign over the American political world as God rules over the universe. It is the cause and the end of all things; everything rises out of it and is absorbed back into it."[4]

Perceptions about the true nature of humans were not, however, consistently positive. Records of debates over the adoption of the Constitution suggest that those who designed our government feared the darker side of human nature even as they sought to establish a just and free society. James Madison, writing *The Federalist* papers, expressed fear that if unrestrained by checks "any individual or group of individuals will tyrannize over others."[5] In defining tyranny in *The Federalist, No. 47,* he states that "the accumulation of all powers, legislative, executive, and judiciary, in the same hands, whether of one, a few, or many, may justly be pronounced the very definition of tyranny."[6] Hamilton expressed the same thought more tersely: "Give all power to the many, they will oppress the few. Give all power to the few, they will oppress the many."[7]

Balance of Powers

According to Madison, the creation of a form of government that would ensure the rights of its citizens against tyranny required the satisfying of two conditions: 1) "The accumulation of all powers, legislative, executive, and judiciary, in the same hands, whether of one, a few, or many, and whether hereditary, self-appointed, or elective, must be avoided"[8]; and 2) "Factions must be so controlled that they do not succeed in acting adversely to the rights of other citizens or to the permanent and aggregate interests of the community."[9]

To avoid the accumulation of powers, our government was structured with separate and independent executive, legislative and judicial branches, and with the familiar system of checks and balances that flows from that division of responsibility. For the framers of the Constitution, control of factions was a knottier problem. According to Madison, a faction is "a number of citizens, whether amounting to a majority or a minority of the whole, who are united and actuated by some common impulse of passion, or of interest, adverse to the rights of other citizens, or to the permanent and aggregate interests of the community."[10]

Madison maintained that factions could be controlled not by controlling their formation, which would be antithetical to the philosophy of a free society, but by controlling their effects. For a minority faction, control of effect may be accomplished by "the republican principle" of voting. Thus the majority can vote down the minority. Limitation of a majority faction, on the other hand, depends on the development of an electorate that is "numerous, extended, and diverse in interests."[11]

Over the years, the American electorate has come to expect factional debate, and the delays that debate creates, whenever Congress considers important legislation. For better or worse, debate and delay have become important parts of our representative democracy. More than anything else, our laws appear to be the result of a seemingly endless process of bargaining, negotiation and compromise among competing powers and factions.

The "Free Market of Ideas"

Tension between the unbounded freedom of the individual and the "permanent and aggregate interests of the community" continues. It is true that Madison and his colleagues failed to find a way to resolve that tension. Today factions abound, although in most instances the diversity of the population does tend to mitigate the impact of any single group. Yet the tension that creates the balance and the ambiguity that requires the renegotiation of the balance in every age have resulted in a government of remarkable resiliency.

What role do libraries play in this complex system of checks and balances? In maintaining the balance of power that protects individual rights, this country has always relied on a free market of ideas in which individuals may pick and choose among competing, even conflicting concepts. Freedom of speech and freedom of the press guarantee the right of an individual, or even a faction, to express diverse and sometimes disturbing ideas. Libraries ensure that those ideas and the knowledge necessary for scientific, technical and social growth and development remain available and accessible to individual citizens.

Any government that espouses the principle of individual rights and freedoms without providing the means to obtain information necessary to exercise those rights is a sham. A democratic form of government without libraries or some institution that performs the role now performed by libraries is, quite simply, unthinkable.

States' Rights

Many present day "Federalists" maintain that the rights and responsibilities of the states supersede those of the federal government, except in those cases specifically defined in the Constitution. This interpretation of the Constitution is drawn primarily from the Tenth Amendment which states: "The powers not delegated to the United States by the Constitution, nor prohibited by it to the States, are reserved to the States respectively, or to the people."

Those who believe strongly in the principle of states' rights feel that the federal government has systematically encroached on the power of the states and now exercises powers far beyond those envisioned by the founding fathers. This issue is especially important for libraries because it touches on the relative responsibilities of state and federal governments in providing necessary financial support.

Like the balance between individual and community rights, tension and ambiguity permeate this issue. Indeed, the question of the extent of states' rights was one major factor in the Civil War, and it is a concern that continues to worry those now struggling with the "new federalism." While it is clear that the relationship between the state governments and the federal government is open to redefinition and interpretation, it is important to remember that rights and responsibilities are inextricably linked. Moreover, a thorough reading of historical documents reveals that the founding fathers were very careful to delineate and delegate those rights and responsibilities.

Developing a Definition of States' Rights

Our founding fathers were not trusting men. They feared tyranny and were suspicious of government. Their primary concern was for the protection of the rights of the people. Division of power within the federal government itself was one way to control the concentration and possible misuse of power. Division of power between the federal and state governments was another.

In framing the Constitution, the founding fathers were careful to grant certain powers to the federal government, and to reserve all others to the states. But they also gave the federal government the responsibility of providing for the "general welfare." Although this clause has been the focus of extensive debate over the years, it appears to justify federal intervention in cases where state governments are violating the rights of individuals. Perhaps even more significantly, the Tenth Amendment itself conditions the powers reserved to the states by adding the phrase "or to the people."

In *The Federalist,* James Madison expands on this fundamental concern with personal freedoms:

> . . . as far as the sovereignty of the States cannot be reconciled to the happiness of the people, the voice of every good citizen must be, let the former be sacrificed to the latter. How far the sacrifice is necessary, has been shown. How far the unsacrificed residue will be endangered, is the question before us.[12]

Protection of individual rights is clearly the chief responsibility of the government, and when there is a conflict between the state governments and the federal government, it is the federal government that makes the final determination. One may argue that the situation should be other than it is, but the facts are clear.

Implications for Libraries and Information Services

The charge that our federal government has grown through the usurpation of individual and states' rights is difficult to prove. It may have evolved in a manner specifically different from that envisioned by Madison and the others. It may be stronger than some would like at the present time. Nevertheless, the power to "conclude on the whole" that has been exercised in federal laws and judicial decisions concerning slavery, working conditions, voting rights, civil rights and individual freedoms was established in the earliest days of the government. The federal government was never meant to be an equal among equals. It was intended to be the sovereign government.

This suggests that the federal government is operating in an appropriate and constitutional capacity when it provides financial support for health care, educational assistance and libraries. Of course, tension and ambiguity persist, and decisions may very well be made that would limit federal government intervention in these areas. But these decisions will be made more on the basis of economic considerations and short term political interests than on constitutional requirements.

Property Rights

Among the individual rights protected by our government is the right to own property. In recent years, as information has come to be viewed as a commodity, issues arising from the conflict between individual right of ownership and federal responsibility to provide for the general economic welfare have become particularly important for libraries and other information providers.

Although the application of these issues to the library area is a relatively new development resulting in part from recent technological innovations, property rights have been a source of tension throughout the history of our nation. Notably, the right to own property was not included directly in either the Declaration of Independence or in the Bill of Rights. In fact, the familiar "natural rights" of "life, liberty and property," were changed by Jefferson in the Declaration of Independence to the "unalienable rights" of "life, liberty and the pursuit of happiness."

In using "pursuit of happiness" Jefferson did more than provide us with a broader, more encompassing term. He also made a clear distinction between protection of rights of property and protection of the diversity of faculties of men from which the rights of property originate. According to Madison, "The protection of these faculties is the first object of government. From the protection of different and unequal faculties of acquiring property, the possession of different degrees and kinds of property immediately results; and from the influence of these on the sentiments and views of the respective proprietors, ensues a division of the society into different interests and parties."[13]

Thus the irony and tension are built into the very fabric of our nation, for the government is charged with protecting those rights that result in the creation of factions. Yet the goal remains, however steeped in ambiguity and paradox, "To secure the public good and private rights against the danger of . . . faction, and at the same time to preserve the spirit and the form of popular government."[14]

Even at the time, however, Jefferson recognized the primacy of individual freedoms and potential that the "exercise of property rights might so interfere with the rights of the individual that the Government, without whose assistance the property rights could not exist, must intervene, not to destroy individualism, but to protect it."[15]

Changing Relationship Between Public and Private Sectors

In observing the shifting American social structure some 70 years later, Alexis de Tocqueville noted, "In democratic societies between these two extremes [of wealth and poverty] there is an innumerable crowd who are much alike, who, though not exactly rich nor yet quite poor, have enough property to want order and not enough to excite envy."[16]

Part of the balance that had been achieved by the mid-19th century was derived from the ever-expanding western frontier that provided land and opportunity to all willing to reach out for it. Shortly after de Tocqueville's observations, another economic force began to move across the American landscape. Fueled by the new nation's vast supply of natural resources and raw materials, the Industrial Revolution changed us from an agricultural to an industrial society and left massive social changes in its wake.

The role of the federal government with respect to property rights began to evolve as well. Infant industries were born, and while a laissez-faire approach was generally recommended by the federal government, the government also extended substantial assistance to the private sector. Tariffs were imposed to give United States industries a competitive edge, and subsidies in the form of loans and outright grants were provided to some developing industries.

As some corporations grew in strength, the balance began to shift. Individuals found their freedoms threatened not by big government, but by big businesses that controlled the lives of millions of Americans. By 1932 small businesses had been squeezed to the point that some 600 corporations controlled two thirds of American industry. This situation caused Franklin Roosevelt to predict that the country was "steering a steady course toward economic oligarchy, if we are not there already."[17]

In 1974 the U.S. Internal Revenue Service reported that 2% of the nation's corporations were responsible for 79.8% of the receipts. This suggests that, in spite of government regulation, the trend toward larger corporate entities continues. Moreover, this trend has been accompanied by a growing number of multi-national corporations whose activities influence worldwide economic conditions.

Federal Responsibility

Many corporations, both small and large, are now involved in information delivery in one way or another. The tension between the private and public sectors constitutes the most important set of issues involved in federal information policies. Within this context, it is imperative to remember that the primary responsibility of the federal government is to maintain balance and to protect the fundamental rights of the individual. Tension and ambiguity are probably more apparent in this context than in any other discussed here. The balance between warring rights and responsibilities will not be easily achieved.

ECONOMIC CONDITIONS AND PRINCIPLES

While political theory provides the philosophical basis for our form of government, the balances that are struck among apparently conflicting values are both the result of and the cause of economic trends. Economic conditions and principles are a powerful force in creating the environment in which libraries exist, and they have a clear impact on the federal government itself.

At the 1979 White House Conference on Library and Information Services, some major goals for library development were enunciated. These were: "to reshape library and information services to serve the people in more useful ways, to maintain local control of these services, and to insist on more economy and accountability from the institutions that provide the services."[18] Since 1979 these concerns have grown and have been reflected in a clear move toward fiscal and political conservatism.

In recent years, the nation has suffered from the twin evils of inflation and recession. Citizens have responded at the local level by limiting the taxing capacity of local governments, thereby diminishing their ability to provide services. This trend started in California with the passage of Proposition 13 in 1978, but has since spread across the country. The results of these tax-cutting initiatives are well-documented elsewhere.

At the federal level, programs have been reduced, consolidated and, in some cases, eliminated. Funding agencies that have been instrumental in providing support for the development and operation of libraries have found their budgets cut severely, and some are even facing termination. No matter how one interprets the trends, there are some economic principles that are generally agreed upon and that affect the government role in providing services. Most notable among these is the nature of public and private goods.

Public vs. Private Goods

A pure public good is generally defined as a good or service that has two essential characteristics: relative efficiency through joint consumption and relative inefficiency when members of the public purchase the product as individual agents. Society as a whole is expected to benefit from "public goods." The most commonly used example of a pure public good is national defense.

A private good, on the other hand, is one that is generally purchased and consumed by an individual. Characteristics of private goods are: they can be provided in divisible units; benefits are not interrelated; and exclusive purchase by individuals is possible. An automobile would be considered a private good.

Although many people think of governments as providing only public goods, that is not the case. The nature of the good is not dependent on the agency (public or private) that makes it available. Some examples of private goods provided or distributed by public agencies include postal service, parking facilities and, in some states, liquor store products.

While the justification for government intervention is more obvious in some instances than in others, it is generally felt that the government is justified in intervening in the marketplace when the provision of specific goods or services contains a collective interest. Sometimes this collective interest is described as "efficiency." That is, governmental units provide a mechanism whereby individuals can act jointly, thereby obtaining more goods and services per dollar than each could acquire by acting independently.

Efficiency alone, however, is not an adequate justification for public intervention in the marketplace. Some individuals obtain the benefits of joint action by entering into voluntary cooperative groups. Private clubs, food co-ops, subscription fire departments and subscription libraries are examples of some of these cooperative arrangements. To be classified as a public good, a product or service must be thought of as providing widespread social benefit as well.

Most governmental services are neither pure public nor pure private goods, but in fact contain elements of both. Education, for instance, provides direct benefits to the individual and exclusion is clearly possible. (One has only to look at private schools.) On the other hand, education is thought of as providing significant benefits to society as a whole by promoting a more enlightened and productive citizenry. This benefit to society as a whole is considered a "spillover effect."

Spillover effects, or externalities, are difficult to define. Costs and benefits that accrue to society are difficult to quantify and are frequently indistinguishable from those that accrue to individuals.

Two additional arguments are used to justify public funding of intermediate public goods such as public libraries. The first of these is that if fees were charged to cover the full cost of the service, some consumers would buy less than is in their true best interest. Second, provision of some services can alter the distribution of income, thereby permitting low income individuals to receive critical goods or services such as food, medical care and education.

Limitations of Public Goods Theory

Although the economic theory of public goods is clearly essential in establishing a conceptual framework for an analysis of the federal role in library development, its utility is limited. An analysis of library activities solely on this basis, for instance, would reveal almost no justification for the delivery of information services to businesses or the support of recreational reading or other leisure-time activities. Yet, distinctions among the cultural, educational, informational and recreational aspects of library services are difficult to make and impossible to measure.

Many have argued that reading of any type has educational benefits, while others maintain that information services always contribute to the economic well-being of the country even if the primary benefits accrue to a specific company or individual. Thus, economic principles must be considered along with social value and political reality for purposes of evaluating public programs and establishing justification for federal intervention.

TECHNOLOGICAL TRENDS

While economic conditions are creating one set of pressures for libraries, the development of an information industry is further conditioning the environment in which libraries must operate. Driven by technological change of massive proportions, this industry, or collection of industries, is changing the landscape of our lives. It is altering the way we work, play and make decisions. It is introducing new products and services, and it is finding new ways to produce old products and services.

The impact of these new developments on libraries has been variously interpreted. Some find hope in the prospect of new, more efficient library systems flowing from greater technological capabilities. Others see the demise of the public library as we know it. They fear that private information services will compete with libraries and further erode an already weak funding base.

Development of Information Technology

Information technology, broadly defined, has been around for quite some time. Computers made their debut when Charles Babbage invented the "difference engine" in the mid-19th century, and human beings have been using various tools and techniques to communicate since the dawn of man. Even electronic communication is not new. The telegraph appeared more than 150 years ago, and the telephone is more than 100 years old.

Nevertheless, recent developments have revolutionized computer and communications technologies and have resulted in what has been called the fourth great communication invention.[19] The first was the invention of writing, the second was the invention of the alphabet, and the third was the application of movable type to printing. This last technological advance is considered by many historians to have been instrumental in the rise of the middle class, the development of modern governmental structures and the birth of the Reformation.

The "Fourth Era"

With advances in telecommunications and micro-electronic technology, we are entering the fourth great technological era. This new era is characterized by the ability to store and retrieve vast amounts of information and the capacity to interact with it, to manipulate it and to re-create it in different forms. All of this is made possible by the computer, especially as it has evolved since the invention of the silicon chip. This small, quarter-inch piece of silicon now contains as many as 100,000 integrated transistors. Since 1953, the size of main computer memory has shrunk 800 times, and it is continuing to shrink at the same fast rate.[20] In 1983 the Nippon Corp. of Japan announced that it plans to produce individual memory chips that can contain more than 1 billion bits of information by 1987.

This, however, is only the beginning. Many scientists talk about the development of computer memory at the molecular level within the foreseeable future. In addition, computer circuitry (the part of the computer responsible for the speed of operation) is also undergoing revolutionary change. Already computer circuits built on new principles have demonstrated a switching rate faster than 20 trillionths of a second.[21]

Cost Effectiveness

Another element that is fundamental to the use of computers is cost. Here, too, the trend is clear—more power for less money. The cost of electronic logic and memory has been falling at a rate of 25% to 30% a year, compounded over the last two decades. Storage technology costs have been decreasing by 40% a year and communications costs by about 11%. Satellite costs have also fallen by 40% annually.[22] Even now small home computers are available for less than $100.

Computers can already offer a relatively inexpensive alternative to rising labor costs, and they have become common in the workplace. Moreover, most information machines consume very little energy, and the primary natural resource needed to build the silicon chips that comprise the computer's logic circuits is cheap and readily available: sand.[23]

Communications Systems

Communications systems, too, are changing rapidly and are becoming increasingly indistinguishable from computer systems. Thus we are seeing the growth of massive "telecomputing" networks. Digital information may now be transmitted using the electromagnetic radio spectrum (radio, television, microwave) or some form of telephone line or cable.

The application of these technologies has created numerous challenges and opportunities. Satellites are now used for video conferencing and document transfer. Cable television is becoming interactive, and 85% of American homes are likely to be connected to cable systems by the end of the decade. American Telephone and Telegraph (AT&T), the largest corporation in the world, is moving aggressively into the information delivery business using existing telephone lines, and various companies are developing viewdata and teletext systems that will bring information directly into the home via cable, broadcast or telephone transmission.

These developments are clearly changing our lives in many ways, and will surely change them more substantially in the future. The most obvious impact to date, however, is not on our personal lives, but upon the economic life of our country and the operation of our institutions.

THE LIBRARY ROLE

Libraries in the 1980s are faced with economic constraints, reduced federal support and far-reaching technological changes. Given this environment, library administrators have a limited number of options. They may cut services, increase productivity or find new sources of revenue. No matter which strategy or combination of strategies libraries use, however, the first step is to do what libraries and other public institutions have always done during times of crisis: re-examine roles, functions and priorities. To establish priorities, it is first necessary to determine the library's proper function.

This is not the first time libraries have found it necessary to rethink their mission. There has always been a delicate balance between the library as an educational institution, the library as a source of recreational reading, the library as a cultural agent, and the library as an information agency.

The public library is, in fact, a multi-purpose agency whose functions have evolved and changed over time. Like other public institutions, libraries respond to the changing needs of the societies in which they exist. In the United States, however, there has always been a gap between the idealized role of the public library and the services actually rendered. This gap has now grown into a chasm that must be bridged. Before a realistic approach to closing the gap can be established, it is necessary to look at roles of the library from several perspectives—rhetoric, reality and technical feasibility.

Rhetoric

The role of the public library has always been defined with almost missionary zeal. Developed and refined for more than a century, the justification for public support of libraries has come to rest on a logical syllogism: democracy is desirable, and it depends on an educated populace; libraries provide the means for educating and informing members of society to pursue both personal and social goals; therefore, libraries are desirable and should receive public support.

Historically, those who have supported public libraries have done so in the belief that they contribute to social stability and progress:

• ". . . it is of paramount importance that the means of general information should be so diffused that the largest possible number of persons should be induced to read and understand questions going down to the very foundations of social order."[24]

• "Libraries are now conducted for the many, not for the few. It is our aim to provide something for everyone who can read."[25]

• "The objectives of the public library . . . in essence are two—to promote enlightened citizenship and to enrich personal life."[26]

• "The library is the best training ground for enlightenment that rational man has ever conceived."[27]

Most recently this message was repeated by delegates to the White House Conference on Library and Information Services:

> WHEREAS, information in a free society is a basic right of any individual, essential for all persons, at all age levels and all economic and social levels, and

> WHEREAS, publicly supported libraries are institutions of education for democratic living and exist to provide information for all,

> THEREFORE BE IT RESOLVED, that the White House Conference on Library and Information Services hereby affirms that all persons should have free access, without charge or fee to the individual, to information in public and publicly supported libraries, and

BE IT FURTHER RESOLVED, that the White House Conference on
Library and Information Services advocates the formation of a National
Information Policy to ensure the right of access without charge or fee
to the individual to all public and publicly supported libraries for all
persons.[28]

Thus, the library creed affirms that the function of the public library is to provide the means necessary for the educational, informational and recreational development of the individual. It is an essential democratic institution because it provides the information that is necessary for a citizen to participate in an informed way in the political process.

Though philosophically appealing, this assertion of the fundamental role of the public library raises one unavoidable question. Why, if libraries are so essential, are they so unsuccessful in attracting support?

Reality

While the underlying philosophy has an egalitarian ring to it, regular users of public libraries have been characterized as "an elite." This term was originally used by Berelson in his landmark study, *The Library's Public,* a volume published in 1949 as part of the *Public Library Inquiry* series. Berelson's findings of 30 years ago have been reinforced by a continuing string of user studies, making his study as valid today as it was at the time.

Briefly, it found that 10% of the adults borrowing books accounted for 98% of all circulation, and that 10% of those frequenting the library were responsible for 95% of the visits. Berelson also noted that active library users were not typical of the population as a whole. They were generally better educated, had a higher income and enjoyed greater social prestige.[29]

A study conducted by the Gallup organization in 1975 found that while 51% of Americans aged 18 and over had visited a public library in the last year, only 9% could be considered "heavy users." In fact, 72% of the population was found to have used the library either "not at all" or "lightly." Moreover, the typical "heavy" user was found to be 18 to 34 years of age, college educated, living in a household with children under 18, and a resident of the eastern part of the United States.[30]

In an effort to determine the role of the library in providing information, as contrasted with providing books, a study of *Information Needs of Urban Residents* was conducted in 1973. It discovered that "only three percent of respondents overall used a library to obtain information on their most important problems."[31] Additional information needs surveys have generated similar findings, and the 1975 Gallup study found that most library users still come to the public library to borrow books, read magazines and consult reference materials.

As noted earlier, the information society appears to be upon us. Xerox, IBM and the postal service all claim to be in the "information business"; and television, radio, newspapers and cable companies all make a claim to protecting our right to know. Many assert (using various methods of counting) that over 50% of our country's gross national product is now derived from information-related activities. Whether we choose to accept that figure or not, it is clearly true that there are a lot of people doing a lot of work under the general rubric of "information."

The real role of public libraries in this new information environment is not clear. Based on the findings outlined above, however, it is obvious that libraries are not the only guardians of liberty, and their position as primary dispensors of education and information is largely mythical.

Libraries do, however, make a unique and significant contribution that justifies public support. They are political as well as social institutions, and libraries do more than educate or inform those using them. In many ways they are and always have been symbols of continuity and social order. They embody the cultural, social, political and economic history of a society. They transmit the ideas, the hopes, the successes and failures of a people. They tell us where we came from and who we are. They are the custodians of value. While it is undoubtedly true that not every voter goes into a library to research an issue prior to voting on it, it is equally true that every voter can.

This role is one that is performed by no other institution. It is unprofitable and without immediately measurable results. It is a public good in every sense of the word. The history of a people is indivisible and nonexcludable, although exclusion from access to it is conceivable. It has not, however, attracted massive amounts of financial support.

Technological Feasibility

The current library dilemma is further exacerbated by the emerging information technologies noted above. While developments in the computer and communications field can revolutionize the manner in which library functions are performed, they are also creating industries that compete with libraries in the provision of information, education and recreational material. The growth of these technology-based industries is further eroding the traditional base of public library support.

Even at the most basic level, library service patterns are being altered. Libraries were originally formed to provide access to books. Many people still define libraries in terms of their book stock, and the vast majority of people visiting libraries do so to borrow or read a book, magazine or other printed material. Yet libraries are not the principal providers of books.

Competing Book Services

Despite the proliferation of radio, television, cable and other media that clang and flash in the night, book publishing has continued to grow over the last two decades. From 1964 to 1980, the number of new titles and editions produced each year grew from 20,542 to 42,377.[32] In recent years, income from book sales has also continued to increase, but the increase has been due more to a rise in prices than a greater volume of sales. For example, from 1976 to 1981, domestic dollar sales for the book publishing industry increased 70.6%, while the total number of volumes sold increased only 19.2%. This slow growth rate has not held true for all book categories, however. Mass market paperback sales almost tripled from 1972 to 1981, while book club sales also experienced a significant increase.[33]

The number of book outlets has also grown. From 1970 to 1980, the total number of bookstores grew 71%, with specialty stores showing the fastest growth. A 1975 survey of American reading habits found that almost one out of three people acquired the last book they read from a friend or relative, while 24% purchased it at a bookstore and only 12% borrowed it from a library.[34]

These data indicate that even in the traditional area of book distribution, libraries have intense competition. Recreational reading is easily and cheaply available, and special interest publications are growing. Moreover, economic constraints are making it increasingly difficult for public libraries to buy more than a small percentage of the titles published each year.

Data Bases and Information Networks

At the same time, advances in computer handling and telecommunications have led to the development of networks that contribute to resource sharing. At one level, the quantum leaps in technological development have provided the basis for enormous economies of scale in performing traditional library functions. Shared cataloging, for instance, is now a reality in many libraries. One spinoff of shared cataloging is the creation of a bibliographic control capability. Though still far from complete, many hope that ultimately there will be a national system of bibliographic control that will enable library users to locate a title no matter where it is housed.

At another level, these technological innovations have led to the development of an entirely new product, the computerized data base. This may consist of either bibliographic citations, abstracts of longer documents, or full text. As of early 1983, there were over 1300 data bases available online, and some information was available only in this format.[35]

Some forecasters have predicted that if the rate of change in computer and communications technologies continues, with continuing reductions in size, speed and cost, the entire contents of the Library of Congress will be readily available to every individual in the country by the end of the century. Even now, using video disc technology read by a laser, the entire contents of the Library of Congress could be stored on 200 feet of shelving—that is, on one wall of a large room.

The potential consequences of these technical developments for libraries are staggering. They point to an erosion of the traditional functions of the library, accompanied by the growth and development of new information services and resources. The gap between the rhetoric and the reality has always existed, but has grown wider during the last decade, a period characterized by increased technological development and a diminished ability of the local government to provide continuing financial support for public services.

THE FEDERAL MANDATE

In spite of the fact that information is generally considered to be a national resource, the move to greater local control and reduced federal support has raised many questions about the legitimate function of the federal government in this arena. Some of these questions are:

• Is the government assuming a legitimate function of the private sector when it distributes information?

• Under what circumstances should the government create information resources and networks?

• What about the user-fee concept? Is it a viable and appropriate mechanism to pay for the distribution of information after the taxpayer has already supported the acquisition of the data?

• How do we measure the private and public good to be derived by government intervention?

• How do we guide and coordinate private sector and government initiatives?

• To what extent should the federal government subsidize local library services?

Other questions abound, but most flow from the same concern. Given the philosophy that the government should intervene only when the free market fails to operate (a philosophy that is on the ascendency), what are the implications for library development? While it is not the purpose of this book to redefine the basis for our federal government, it is important to examine principles of political theory to determine the degree to which federal intervention in library-related issues is appropriate.

Clearly, some of the items listed above are outside the purview of the federal government. Technological developments, economic trends and the definition of the library's mission are examples of issues that the federal government deals with only tangentially. These do, however, serve to define the environment in which the federal role is acted out. As such they are critically important in any discussion of the federal impact on library and information service development.

Library-Related Activities

Within this context most library-related federal activities fall within four general groupings: data collection and distribution, financial support through grants-in-aid programs, research and demonstration, and planning and policy making.

Like the federal government itself, the federal role in library and information service development is based on tension and ambiguity. Tension arises from conflicting values and creates the need for balance, while ambiguity reveals the need for continuing interpretation of policy.

Historically, the federal government first developed library services to meet its own needs, and it first established information policies and regulations to ensure that information was not controlled or manipulated. This function flows from the principle of individual rights and the practical necessity of providing the information necessary for informed decision making both within the federal government itself and by voters.

Appropriate Federal Roles

The continuation of federal data collection is really not an issue. There are, however, profound issues involved in the degree to which the federal government distributes information that it generates. Here the relative roles of the public and private sectors bump up against each other. Property rights must be considered as well as individual rights. The situation is further complicated by economic trends and political expediencies.

Only recently has the federal government assumed a larger financial responsibility by supporting information-related research and development and by providing grants-in-aid for libraries. Although these functions have been challenged by some as the responsibility of the states rather than the federal government, a careful reading of the Constitution and supporting documents reveals that this type of activity is clearly within the area of federal responsibility. The continuation of funding programs is therefore more an economic decision based on short-term political goals than a policy decision based on established democratic principles.

Planning and policy making is another important area in which the federal government plays a role. The question here is not whether the federal government should set policy but what kind of policy it should set. In reality, the federal government could not avoid setting policy even if it wished. Moreover, as information plays an increasingly important part in all aspects of our social and political life, information policy is sure to become more controversial and much more political in all senses of the word.

Federal data collection and distribution, grants-in-aid programs, research and development, and planning and policy making have all had a significant impact on libraries as we know them. Subsequent chapters will examine the various federal approaches to library development, and explore current and future options for federal involvement in library and information services.

FOOTNOTES

1. Daniel J. Boorstin, *The Republic of Technology* (New York: Harper & Row, 1978).

2. *Ibid.*

3. Carl L. Becker, "Freedom of Speech and Press" in *Readings in American Democracy,* ed. by Gerald Stourzh, Ralph Lerner and H.C. Harlan (New York: Oxford University Press, 1966).

4. Alexis de Tocqueville, *Democracy in America,* ed. by J.P. Mayer (Garden City, NY: Doubleday & Company, Inc., 1969).

5. Robert A. Dahl, *A Preface to Democratic Theory* (Chicago: University of Chicago Press, 1956).

6. *The Federalist,* ed. by Edward Mead Earle (New York: Random House, n.d.), No. 47.

7. Robert A. Dahl, op. cit.

8. *The Federalist,* No. 47.

9. *The Federalist,* No. 10.

10. *The Federalist,* No. 10.

11. Robert A. Dahl, op. cit.

12. *The Federalist,* No. 45.

13. *The Federalist,* No. 10.

14. *The Federalist,* No. 10.

15. Franklin D. Roosevelt, "To Promote the General Welfare" in *Readings in American Democracy,* ed. by Gerald Stourzh, Ralph Lerner and H.C. Harlan (New York: Oxford University Press, 1966).

16. Alexis de Tocqueville, op. cit.

17. Franklin D. Roosevelt, op. cit.

18. *Information for the 1980s: The Final Report of the White House Conference on Library and Information Services, 1979* (Washington, DC: Government Printing Office, 1980).

19. Howard Resnikoff, *Program Report: Information Science and Technology* (Washington, DC: National Science Foundation, 1979).

20. Lewis M. Branscomb, "Library Implications of Information Technology" in *An Information Agenda for the 1980s,* ed. by Carlton C. Rochell (Chicago: American Library Association, 1981).

21. *Ibid.*

22. Carlton C. Rochell, *An Information Agenda for the 1980s, Proceedings of a Colloquium June 17-18, 1980* (Chicago: American Library Association, 1981).

23. Richard Neustadt, unpublished remarks made during the planning period for the White House Conference on Library and Information Services, Washington, DC, 1979.

24. *Report of the Trustees of the Public Library of the City of Boston, July, 1852* in Jesse Shera, *Foundations of the Public Library: The Origins of the Public Library Movement in New England, 1629-1855* (Chicago: University of Chicago Press, 1949).

25. Arthur E. Bostwick, "The Future of Library Work," *ALA Bulletin* 12:51-52.

26. Carleton B. Joeckel, "Questions of a Political Scientist," *ALA Bulletin* 27: 66-69.

27. Elizabeth W. Stone, *Historical Approach to American Library Development: A Chronological Chart.* Occasional Paper No. 83, University of Illinois Graduate School of Library Science, May, 1967.

28. *Information for the 1980s,* op. cit.

29. Bernard Berelson, *The Library's Public* (New York: Columbia University Press, 1949).

30. The Gallup Organization, *The Role of Libraries in America* (Princeton: Gallup, 1975).

31. Edward S. Warner et al., *Information Needs of Urban Residents* (Washington, DC: Office of Education, U.S. Department of Health, Education and Welfare, 1973).

32. *Consumer Media Expenditures 1982-87* (White Plains, NY: Knowledge Industry Publications, Inc., 1983).

33. *Ibid.*

34. The Gallup Organization, op. cit.

35. *Data Base/Electronic Publishing Review and Forecast* (White Plains, NY: Knowledge Industry Publications, Inc., 1983).

3

Federal Data Collection and Distribution

The federal government has been described as a giant information processing machine. In view of the fact that the federal government is the largest information producer and distributor in the country, that assertion is certainly true. The purpose of this chapter, however, is not to describe all federal information-related activities, but to look specifically at the federal role in providing library and other information services directly.

Direct federal information services include the services provided through our great national libraries: the Library of Congress (LC), the National Library of Medicine (NLM) and the National Agricultural Library (NAL). They also include the services provided through the vast network of smaller federal libraries that supports the work of the government. And they include a number of publishing and document distribution services, such as those provided by the Joint Committee on Printing, the Government Printing Office, the Federal Depository System, the National Technical Information Service (NTIS) and other agencies charged with direct distribution of government information.

This chapter will document the activities of the federal government as a consumer, producer and distributor of information. Sections will describe services and issues arising from the operation and management of federal libraries and information distribution services. Policy issues such as the relationship between the federal government and private information firms, the information role of the Office of Management and Budget, and the impact of the Freedom of Information Act and other information-related legislation will be considered in Chapter 6.

LIBRARY OF CONGRESS

Since before the United States was born, our national leaders have displayed a respect for knowledge and an appreciation for the importance of informed decision making. As one of its first acts, the Continental Congress, meeting in Philadelphia in August 1774, arranged with the Library Company of Philadelphia to furnish members with the "use of

such Books as they may have occasion for during their sitting, taking a Receipt for them."
James Madison later described books from Europe as indispensable, and he noted that
lack of information had been "manifest in several important acts of Congress."[1]

Establishment and Early History

When the First Congress of the United States convened at City Hall in New York City
on March 4, 1789, the members were given access to the New York Society Library located
in the same building. On August 16, 1789, a motion was passed "that a committee be appointed to report a catalogue of books necessary for the use of Congress, with an estimate
of the expense, and the best mode of procuring them." On April 24, 1800, President John
Adams signed a bill into law that officially created the Library of Congress. It contained a
provision for the purchase of $5000 worth of books to be used by both houses of Congress.

Since its creation, the Library of Congress has grown steadily in both size and importance. After the British burned the Library in 1814, Congress voted to replace the loss with
Thomas Jefferson's impressive personal collection. In one move, this shifted the scope of the
library from a small functional collection to a comprehensive repository of knowledge.

As the library began to expand, so did those permitted to use its facilities. By 1850,
LC's services were extended to the executive and judiciary branches of government, and to
the diplomatic corps, American colleges and universities, and the American Antiquarian
Society. Its collection had grown to over 50,000 volumes, making it the second-largest
library in the country (Harvard University had 84,000 volumes at the time). It had also
become the first agency of the federal government to participate in a program of "international intellectual cooperation."[2]

In 1851 the Library was once again struck by fire. This time 35,000 volumes were
destroyed, including two thirds of the Thomas Jefferson collection. In the 20 years that
followed, the Library, with major financial support from Congress, embarked on a
massive acquisitions program. By 1869 it contained 175,000 volumes and was the largest
library in the United States.[3] This growth was further spurred by the Copyright Law of
1870, which required that anyone seeking copyright on any piece of printed material send
two copies to the Librarian of Congress within 10 days of publication. In 1897 the
Library's huge and growing collection was housed in the magnificent building that still
stands across from the Capitol.

Role of Library of Congress

Three major principles guiding the development of the Library of Congress emerged
early in its history: 1) it is Congress's library; 2) it is nevertheless committed to providing a
comprehensive collection (as opposed to a narrow, legislative collection); and 3) it provides
access to this collection to many in addition to members of Congress.

Because of these principles, the role of the Library of Congress has always been ambiguous. On the one hand, many members of Congress feel that LC should be just what

its name implies, the Congressional library. On the other hand, most members of the library profession and the scholarly community feel that the Library of Congress should function more formally as our national library. Actually, LC is neither authorized nor funded to function as an official national library. At the same time, the sheer size of its collection and the universal impact of its activities place it in a unique and very powerful position.

The Library of Congress is probably the largest library in the world. Its collection stands at more than 77 million items (including books, manuscripts, periodicals, pamphlets and other materials), and it is growing at the rate of more than 1 million items per year. The size of the Lenin State Library in Moscow is uncertain, but the Bibliothèque Nationale in Paris reports 13 million pieces of material, the British Museum counts 7 million, and Harvard University (now the second-largest library in the United States) contains 8.5 million items.

Fundamental Activities

Collections development, cataloging and reference services continue to be the library's fundamental and most significant activities. These services, in fact, provide the base of operations both within the Library and for nationwide services. Once materials are collected and processed, they are used in the Library itself by members of Congress and their staffs, federal employees engaged in official studies for their agencies, members of the press and individual citizens and scholars.

LC extends its service to other libraries through interlibrary loan; photoduplication; the sale of sound recordings released by the Recording Laboratory; the exchange of duplicate materials; and the sale of printed catalog cards, magnetic tapes and book catalogs that provide access to the bibliographic and cataloging work of LC staff. The Library also sponsors a Cataloging-in-Publication program developed in cooperation with American publishers; the National Serials Data Program, which maintains a record of serial titles to which International Standard Serial Numbers (ISSNs) have been assigned; and the research and development of classification systems used by the entire library profession.

Scholarly and Professional Services

Traditionally, the Library of Congress has recognized its implicit national responsibilities to the scholarly world and to the library profession even as it has been careful not to overstep its legislated authority. National activities started around the beginning of the century, when LC began producing and distributing catalog cards. In announcing the new program in 1901, Librarian of Congress Herbert Putnam addressed the mixed responsibilities of the library directly:

> If there is any way in which our National Library may "reach out" from
> Washington, it should reach out. Its first duty is, no doubt, as a legislative
> library to Congress. Its next is as a federal library to aid the executive and
> judicial departments of the government and the scientific undertakings under

government auspices. Its next is that of general research which may be carried
on at Washington . . . But this should not be the limit. There should be
possible also a service to the country at large; a service to be extended
through the libraries which are the local centers of research involving the use
of books.[4]

This "service to the country at large" continued with the development of the Library
of Congress Book Catalog and the National Union Catalog. These programs laid the
groundwork for future library networking activities by developing MAchine-Readable Cataloging (MARC) and making it available to those wishing it.

The approach over the years has been consistent. The Library of Congress develops
the tools it needs to manage its own enormous collection and then makes them available to
others, thereby providing a *de facto* standard and point of departure without imposing a
central authority or predetermined structure. Using this approach, LC has had a massive
influence on nationwide library development.

National Network Activities

The most obvious example of LC's style may be found in the development of nationwide networking activities. Both defenders and detractors of the Library agree that the current range of networking activities is a direct result of the non-interventionist position
taken by LC after the introduction of MARC in the 1960s. Those who feel that greater
centralization of efforts is desirable see this as a shirking of responsibility, while those who
feel that diversity and competition are more significant applaud the Library's position.

Network Advisory Committee

Although the Library of Congress has been reluctant to assume the central role in the
establishment of a "national library network," it has concerned itself with nationwide network development and has supported coordination efforts. In 1976 a Network Advisory
Committee (NAC) to LC's Network Development Office was established. Composed of
representatives of networks throughout the country, NAC was originally formed to explore
cooperative efforts among networks. With funding from the Council on Library Resources
(CLR), NAC met and worked for more than a year to "identify those issues and problems
which must be resolved before the bibliographic component of a national network can be
established."[5]

In 1977 NAC issued a report that addressed a number of important issues including:

• The goals, assumptions and objectives behind the library bibliographic component
of the national network;

• The role of the Library of Congress in the evolving network;

• Tasks which should be performed initially in the developing network;

• The role of authority control of bibliographic records.[6]

The report concluded that authority control and the establishment of standards are difficult but essential issues, that research and development is required to determine the most effective and efficient approaches to the resolution of numerous issues, and that developmental funding would be required to proceed with further planning and implementation.

A management committee was subsequently established to provide overall guidance and direction to program development. A program committee was also appointed to assist in the definition of plans and projects. In November 1978 a joint meeting of the management and program committees was called. The results of this meeting were:

1) Identification of three basic, interrelated areas for further activity:

• design, implementation, and evaluation of a system linking the bibliographic utilities

• determination of which databases would be made available and level of completeness of their records

• design and implementation of a nationwide authority system

2) Expressed need for economic assessment and justification for each project undertaken.[7]

In spite of the avowed intent to cooperate, subsequent studies and numerous meetings of members of the Bibliographic Services Development Program (BSDP) and the Network Advisory Committee and its subcommittees have failed to yield a viable plan of cooperation. As one author who has been intimately involved in these efforts notes: "In spite of these efforts at coordinating networking activities nationwide, there appears at this time to be a politically and economically disjointed library networking community."[8]

Other Network Activities

Other efforts undertaken by the Library of Congress to promote cooperative networking activities include the COMARC (COoperative MARC) project and CONSER (CONversion of SERials). COMARC, an attempt to employ cooperative efforts from several libraries for the retrospective conversion of LC records, was abandoned in 1978 for lack of funding and inadequate productivity. CONSER, an attempt to amass a data base of serials records, was funded by CLR and required the cooperative efforts of the Library of Congress and OCLC (now the Online Computer Library Center). Initial plans provided for the transfer of CONSER to the Library of Congress in 1977. As of early 1983, this had not occurred, and the system was still supported by OCLC.

In 1980 the Office of Processing Services was reorganized into Processing Systems, Networks and Automation Planning. With this change, the Network Development Office was combined with the Automated Systems Office and given other functions related to the maintenance of MARC communication formats and the accompanying liaison efforts.

In its role as a *de facto* national library, the Library of Congress has joined with the other national libraries, NLM and NAL, in a series of meetings held to increase cooperation and resolve differences in procedures. Some topics that have been discussed include cooperation in building an online name authority file, cooperative acquisitions and cataloging.

Other Activities

LC also houses the Copyright Office, the federal office that administers copyright laws and handles copyright applications. The office currently processes applications for copyright registration at the rate of 10,000 per week, and applications continue to grow in number and complexity as materials are developed in a wider variety of formats. In addition, LC operates the Congressional Research Service (CRS), the research arm of Congress. CRS answers more than 300,000 questions per year and prepares issue briefs on current topics of high interest.

The National Library Service for the Blind and Physically Handicapped provides services to more than 700,000 citizens through a nationwide network of approximately 160 cooperating libraries. In addition, it has programs in research and development, automation, quality control and public education. The American Folklife Center, created in 1976, conducts field work and produces publications, exhibitions and programs intended to educate the American public about folklore, customs and music. The Center for the Book was formed in 1977 to investigate the transmission of human knowledge and to heighten public awareness of the role of books and printing in the diffusion of knowledge. The National Preservation Program conducts research and distributes information on new techniques for preserving and restoring documents.

LC's Influence on Libraries

The Library of Congress appears to be strongest in the areas of technical design and file building. It engages in research and development at the most basic level and establishes standards simply by virtue of the size of its data base. Its attempts to assist in interlibrary coordination have been only moderately successful. They continue, however, and provide at least one forum for debate and discussion.

The Library of Congress is clearly not at this time a national library in the most comprehensive interpretation of that term. It has, in fact, systematically refrained from filling that role. This was made abundantly clear during the discussions concerning a National Periodicals Center, when LC refused to be considered for a central, operational role.

Nevertheless, LC is a formidable agency. Its budget is almost as large as all library grants-in-aid programs put together. Moreover, it continues to grow regardless of the prevailing political philosophies in Congress and the executive branch, and its services reflect that continuing expansion. From the perspective of national library development, never has a federal agency had so much power, or used it so cautiously.

NATIONAL LIBRARY OF MEDICINE

While the Library of Congress is the world's largest library, many feel that the National Library of Medicine is the world's most technically advanced. Originally founded in 1836 as the Library of the Surgeon General's Office, it was renamed the Army Medical Library in 1922 and the Armed Forces Medical Library in 1952. In 1956 it was officially named the National Library of Medicine, when it became an independent administrative unit of the Public Health Service. Its mission is the advancement of the medical and related sciences by the collection, dissemination and exchange of information important to the progress of medicine and public health.[9]

Roles and Responsibilities

Officially designated as a national library, NLM serves as the country's chief medical information source. It is authorized to:

> . . . provide medical library services and on-line bibliographic searching capabilities, such as MEDLINE and TOXLINE, to public and private agencies and organizations, institutions, and individuals. It is responsible for the development and management of a Biomedical Communications Network, applying advanced technology to the improvement of bio-medical communications, and operating a computer-based toxicology information system for the scientific community, industry, and other federal agencies.[10]

NLM has long been a leader in library development, especially in the creative use of computer and communications technologies to extend access to specialized materials. *Index Medicus,* the Library's monthly publication of references to biomedical journals, was initiated in 1879 and its Medical Literature Analysis and Retrieval System (MEDLARS), a computer-based bibliographic system, began operation in 1964.

MEDLARS II now serves more than 2000 institutions, including hospitals, medical schools and universities, research institutions and commercial organizations. Although it provides access to more than 20 data bases, including TOXLINE (Toxicology Information Online), CHEMLINE (Chemical Dictionary Online), RTECS (Registry of Toxic Effects of Chemical Substances) and POPLINE (Population and Family Planning Information Online), the bulk of the MEDLARS searches (2.2 million in 1982) are conducted on MEDLINE (MEDLARS Online).

Plans are now underway to develop MEDLARS III, which is intended to:

> . . . improve, extend, and integrate both the Library's internal operations (such as technical processing of books and journals) and its external network services. In this latter category, MEDLARS III will provide new capabilities to assist the nation's health science libraries in the creation of bibliographic

records, retrieval of bibliographic and text information, access to national holdings and location information, and ordering and delivery of documents.[11]

Lister Hill Center

The long-planned Lister Hill Center, opened in 1980, houses the Lister Hill National Center for Biomedical Communications. This division is the research and development component of NLM. While it has existed as an organization since 1968, the move to the new building provides it with new visibility and greater opportunities. The purpose of the Lister Hill National Center for Biomedical Communications is to create new biomedical communication systems and networks. The emphasis is on experimentation and research.

One system developed by the Lister Hill Center and released in 1980 is the Integrated Library System (ILS). This computer-based system provides health-sciences libraries of all sizes with software needed to improve their services, to manage their collections and to promote resource sharing. The first version of ILS was composed of four basic elements: a Master Bibliographic File (MBF), the Circulation Subsystem, the Serials Check-in Subsystem, and the Online Catalog Access Subsystem. Planned enhancements of the ILS include: serials control, cataloging, authority control, acquisitions, generalized network access and patron interface.

In 1980 the Lister Hill Center also began to develop an experimental system designed to store, retrieve and display documents acquired by the library. The three major components of this project are research in document capture, data transfer and storage, and document display.

Other Services

In addition to the activities described above, NLM coordinates a Regional Medical Library (RML) program, a national network of 11 regional libraries, over 100 resource libraries and approximately 3000 affiliated libraries. Each of the regional medical libraries is responsible for coordinating information delivery services in its region.

The RML network handles more than 2 million interlibrary loans per year. In 1980 NLM awarded nearly $3 million in grants to regional and resource libraries participating in the RML program. This Extramural Grants Program is funded through the Medical Library Assistance Act. (See Chapter 4.)

Research and Development

In contrast to the Library of Congress, which collects, catalogs and provides access to virtually the entire universe of human knowledge, the National Library of Medicine provides a highly specialized set of services to a specific clientele. Given such a focused body of information and the professional needs of its clients, the National Library of Medicine has concentrated more than any other library on developing sophisticated communications systems that will ensure the delivery of information quickly and efficiently.

To achieve speed and accuracy in information delivery, NLM has committed a large amount of funding to research and development. The results of this research and development have then been incorporated into the day-to-day service activities of NLM, thereby providing justification for more research. Service innovations are also apparent in the Regional Medical Library program, which brings information and materials closer to the information user.

NLM's Influence on Libraries

Although NLM is slightly outside the more general library sphere, its influence should not be underestimated. Internal services, networking, education and research at the National Library of Medicine are all services that are on the leading edge in library system development. Although NLM does contribute directly to general library development by exporting many of its systems and designs, its most significant contribution may be its stature as a model. Perhaps more than any other library, NLM has shown the library community that "it can be done."

TECHNICAL INFORMATION SYSTEMS/NATIONAL AGRICULTURAL LIBRARY

Not as well known as the National Library of Medicine, the National Agricultural Library is our country's other official national library. Founded with the Department of Agriculture under the Organic Act of 1862, NAL is younger and smaller than NLM. According to the legislation, its purpose is "to acquire and diffuse among the people of the United States useful information on subjects connected with agriculture in the most general and comprehensive sense of the word."

Technical Information Systems

In 1978 the National Agricultural Library became a part of the newly established Technical Information Systems (TIS) within the Science and Education Administration (SEA) of the U.S. Department of Agriculture (USDA). Under the new configuration, three divisions exist within TIS. The Library Operations Division is responsible for the administration of NAL, the Information Systems Division operates the many computer systems necessary to provide information, and the Educational Resources Division develops programs designed to increase awareness of technical information services available through TIS. The Educational Resources Division is also charged with coordinating the services of TIS and other institutions. Although it is still commonly known as the National Agricultural Library, NAL's official designation is now "Technical Information Systems/ National Agricultural Library."

Library Operations Division

The Library Operations component of TIS/NAL collects, catalogs and maintains a comprehensive, worldwide collection of materials concerning food and agricultural sciences and related USDA needs. It also maintains a complete collection of USDA-produced publications; promotes cooperation among appropriate insitutions; and provides a variety of library services to USDA personnel, other libraries, domestic and foreign researchers and the general public.

Information Systems Division

Like NLM, NAL has developed a family of data bases. In the TIS/NAL system, these data services are currently coordinated by the Information Services Division. The largest of the NAL data bases is Agriculture On-Line Access (AGRICOLA), established in 1973 and now available commercially through online vendors. With more than 1.4 million citations, it is the largest agriculture bibliographic data base in the world. Other NAL data bases include:

• A continuing inventory of ongoing and completed research projects (CRIS);

• An Agriculture Energy File (AEF) that contains information about energy research projects related to agriculture conducted by federal, state and non-governmental institutions (including results of such projects when available);

• A system that documents and reports on the level of effort devoted to a variety of extension activities conducted by federal and state extension professionals (EMIS);

• A system that documents and reports on the federal research resources being used for specific problems, commodities and disciplines in different geographic areas (PARIS);

• A Current Awareness Literature Service (CALS) designed to keep scientists aware of published developments in food, agriculture and related scientific disciplines; and

• Various other specialized bibliographic files designed to meet the needs of research, extension and teaching professionals and organizations.

TIS/NAL is also the largest contributor to the International Information Systems for the Agriculture Sciences and Technology (AGRIS). Computer compatibility with this system was developed through cooperative agreements with the Agency for International Development. Participation in AGRIS has enabled TIS to include some foreign materials in the AGRICOLA file since 1981.

Regional Document Delivery System

The National Agricultural Library also coordinates the Regional Document Delivery System, a cooperative effort with land-grant libraries instituted to ensure delivery of information to USDA field personnel. In addition to providing requested information through a six-region structure, TIS is working with land-grant colleges to microfilm their agricultural publications.

Educational Resources Division

With the initiation of the Educational Resources Division, TIS has begun an aggressive education and training program designed to increase general awareness of services provided by TIS/NAL. In addition, workshops and other training activities are teaching researchers, librarians and others around the country how to make better use of TIS systems and services.

NAL's Influence on Libraries

To date, NAL has functioned mainly as a service agency within the Department of Agriculture environment. Through the reorganization and expansions that have taken place since 1978, it was hoped that TIS/NAL would be able to provide a broader base of service similar in scope to the range of services offered by the National Library of Medicine. In early 1983, however, a blue ribbon panel of federal library leaders found that NAL's services had actually declined in recent years:

> . . . because of declining resources, poor management, and reorganizations within the Department of Agriculture, [NAL] has suffered a steady decline in services, both to its Department and to its users in the nation and in the community of international agricultural information users. Once a leader in automation and development of online information services, NAL [has] dropped behind.[12]

The panel went on to recommend a number of changes, including increases in funding and staffing, greater use of modern technology, and the establishment of an agricultural information network and resource sharing program. If these proposals are implemented, NAL may once again emerge as a key provider of international agricultural information services, and as an important source of information and data services to the library community at large.

NATIONAL ARCHIVES AND RECORDS SERVICE

The National Archives and Records Service (NARS) is not really a national library. In fact, the American Library Association, in reporting on federal programs, does not even list it as a "library program." It lists NARS, instead, as "library related." Nevertheless, the National Archives is included here because it is an important national service, and because it has had a profound impact on the functions of the Library of Congress.

Establishment and History

The National Archives was established in 1934. Title 44 of the *United States Code* authorizes the National Archives and Records Service to perform a variety of functions related to the preservation, use and disposition of the records of the United States Government.

Before the establishment of NARS, many of these functions were performed by the Library of Congress. In fact, as late as the early 1950s, LC was still the official "keeper of the Presidential Papers." At that time, LC responsibility for presidential manuscripts from Washington to Coolidge was ended, and presidential papers since Hoover were designated for storage in a memorial library under the supervision of NARS. Even the Declaration of Independence and the Constitution were removed to the Archives at that time.

Functions and Responsibilities

At present NARS is located in the General Services Administration, and it is charged with preserving and making available for further government use and for private research the nation's records of enduring value. The National Archives is also the agency responsible for reviewing all government documents to decide which should be preserved. These documents are then cataloged and made available to researchers. In conjunction with this responsibility, NARS provides reference services at the National Archives Building and its branches in regional records centers.

In addition to the archival program, NARS' other activities include: records management, maintenance of federal archives and records centers, publication of laws and presidential documents, and administration of presidential libraries. The records management function allows federal agencies to seek assistance from NARS to improve management of government records and to assure appropriate disposition of inactive records.

Noncurrent records of federal agencies and historically valuable regional records are stored at Federal Archives and Records Centers. These centers also provide access to materials as needed.

NARS is responsible for several important publications containing legislation and other official information from the Congress and the president. These include: *United States Statutes at Large,* the *Federal Register,* the *Code of Federal Regulations,* the *Weekly Compilation of Presidential Documents,* the *Public Papers of the Presidents,* and the *United States Government Manual.*

As an extension of its responsibility for the preservation of presidential documents, NARS administers all presidential libraries. Generally, funds to construct a presidential library are privately raised, but operating funds are provided by a congressional appropriation through NARS.

Through its various storage and records-management activities, NARS is responsible for preserving, cataloging and maintaining public and institutional access to historical documents and important government records. In doing so, NARS performs a key library function for the nation.

FEDERAL LIBRARIES AND INFORMATION CENTERS

In addition to operating the three national libraries and the National Archives, the federal government provides information to its agencies through a plethora of specialized libraries. The magnitude of federal library activity may be seen in Table 3.1, drawn from a survey of federal libraries conducted by the National Center for Education Statistics for FY 1978 (the most recent year for which there is complete data).

Table 3.1 Federal Library Survey, Fiscal Year 1978

	Three National Libraries	All Other Federal Libraries[1]
Circulation (number of items)	2,290,260	38,467,776
Book volumes at end of year	20,782,169	35,862,969
Periodicals	5,396,354	5,201,660
Operating expenditures	$185,470,912	$331,070,595
Employees (full-time-equivalent)	5,194	15,002

[1]Number of libraries: Universe = 2142; respondents = 1880.
Source: National Center for Education Statistics, U.S. Department of Education.

Federal Library Committee

Activities of the numerous libraries operated by individual federal agencies are coordinated to a limited extent through the Federal Library Committee (FLC). Founded in 1965, FLC is a cooperative organization of more than 2600 federal libraries. According to its original mandate, FLC's purpose is to concentrate the intellectual resources in the federal library and library-related information community: "to achieve better utilization of library resources and facilities; to provide more effective planning, development, and operation of federal libraries; to promote an optimum exchange of experience, skill, and resources; to promote more effective service to the nation at large."

To achieve these objectives, FLC work groups are working to:

• Consider policies and problems relating to federal libraries;

• Evaluate existing federal library programs and resources;

• Determine priorities among library issues requiring attention;

• Examine the organization and policies for acquiring, preserving and making information available;

• Study the need for and potential of technological innovation in library practices; and

• Study library budgeting and staffing problems, including the recruiting, education, training and remuneration of librarians.

Federal Library and Information Network

One of the most successful of FLC's programs is the Federal Library and Information Network (FEDLINK). FEDLINK is a cooperative program established to reduce costs and increase services available through participating federal libraries. It accomplishes its objectives by providing a computer-based network for shared cataloging, interlibrary loan, acquisitions and information retrieval. It acts as a broker for the Online Computer Library Center (OCLC), Bibliographic Retrieval Services (BRS) and Dialog Information Retrieval Service, and arranges for other data base services upon request. In addition, the MARC data bases are being extended to include records contributed by the Government Printing Office through FEDLINK, and FEDLINK is considering the establishment of its own data base.

According to its original guidelines, FEDLINK was established to:

1. Expedite and facilitate on-line data base services among federal libraries and information centers;

2. Develop plans for the expansion of such services to federal libraries and information centers;

3. Promote cooperation and utilization of the full potential of networks and technologies to institutions and provide for formal relationships between library and information networks and the FEDLINK membership;

4. Serve as the major federal library and information cooperative system in the emerging national library and information service network; and

5. Promote education, research, and training in network services and new library and information technology for the benefit of federal libraries and information centers.

Libraries linked through FEDLINK and represented by the Federal Library Committee are significant in scope. Many contain unique documents and information that would be difficult, if not impossible, to locate elsewhere. Together, these libraries comprise an important national information resource that contributes both to governmental decision making and to the general availability of important data.

FEDLINK's services are also important when viewed from the perspective of the federal role in library and information services. In many ways, they provide a basic infrastructure of information. Taken as a whole, they represent a significant role and responsibility of the federal government. In the early 1980s, however, federal agencies that provide information services have come under increasing attack from groups that argue for a more limited federal role in information distribution. An analysis of the appropriate role of the federal government in this area appears in Chapter 6.

Other Federal Data Bases

Individual government departments and agencies also operate their own information files and data bases. The following paragraphs provide brief descriptions of some of the federal data bases and services that are currently available to professional groups and the general public.* The descriptions are adapted from the government publication *Federal Information Sources and Systems.*

Patent Search Files (U.S. Patent and Trademark Office)

This system is designed to provide a comprehensive collection of U.S. and foreign patents to be used by patent examiners, patent attorneys and inventors in search of information related to filing and/or prosecuting patent applications; by individuals seeking a specific patent; and by the general public in search of technical information. Information is distributed in paper form, and public access to the files is available at the Patent and Trademark Office's Public Search Room.

NTIS Bibliographic Data Base (Department of Commerce)

This file contains more than 1 million bibliographic citations of federally sponsored research, development and engineering reports; computer products; and inventions available for licensing. Selected state and local government reports are also included. The Bibliographic Data File is one means through which NTIS fulfills its responsibility to distribute information products from U.S. government agencies. The service's magnetic data tapes may be leased annually, and tapes back to 1964 may be acquired. The file is also available through commercial online information systems.

Currently, there is conflict between NTIS and private sector information firms concerning the appropriate role of the federal government in marketing government publications. NTIS is discussed at greater length below.

Census Bureau Population Statistics System (Department of Commerce)

This file consists of data collected in the decennial censuses. The data are used by Congress, by the executive branch and by the general public in the development and evaluation of economic and social programs. Information is available on computer tape or in print form.

Library General Information Survey System (LIBGIS) (Department of Education)

This system is designed to collect, process, analyze and disseminate data on all types of libraries; on educational broadcasting facilities and programs; and, occasionally, on

---

*For more information on government data bases available online, see *Online Search Strategies,* edited by Ryan E. Hoover (White Plains, NY: Knowledge Industry Publications, Inc., 1982).

museums. The LIBGIS surveys are available in print reports and on magnetic computer tapes. Theoretically, the data are updated every two to five years, but reduced funding may make it difficult for LIBGIS to maintain this schedule.

Educational Resources Information Center (ERIC) (Department of Education)

ERIC is a nationwide, decentralized, online information network for acquiring, selecting, abstracting, indexing, storing, retrieving and disseminating the most significant and timely education-related reports. It consists of a coordinating staff in Washington, DC and 16 clearinghouses operated in conjunction with professional organizations across the country. The abstract journal is available by subscription from the Government Printing Office. Most documents may be purchased either in microfiche or paper form.

Justice Retrieval Inquiry System (JURIS)
(Department of Justice)

This computerized legal research system provides fast, comprehensive and incisive retrieval of case law, statutory law and internal departmental materials. Used by Department of Justice lawyers, this system is not available to the public because of the expense and contractual restrictions on dissemination of data held under license.

NASA Library Network (NALNET) (National Aeronautics and Space Administration)

NALNET is an online network that connects the NASA libraries located at headquarters and 11 research centers, to provide access to the more than 180,000 books and 6000 journals located throughout the system.

Information Analysis Centers

In addition to the libraries and information centers described above, the federal government also operates approximately 100 Information Analysis Centers (IACs). These centers differ from federal libraries in scope and purpose. Although each IAC offers a different range of services, they tend to focus on a specific, somewhat narrow range of information and to provide analysis as well as access.

Information Analysis Centers are a relatively recent phenomenon, with 70% of them appearing since 1960. The National Referral Center defines an IAC as:

> . . . a formally structured organizational unit specifically (but not necessarily exclusively) established for the purpose of acquiring, selecting, storing, retrieving, evaluating, analyzing, and synthesizing a body of information and/or data in a clearly-defined specialized field or pertaining to a specific mission with the intent of compiling, digesting, repackaging, or otherwise organizing and presenting pertinent information and/or data in a form most authoritative, timely, and useful to a society of peers and management.[13]

Information Analysis Centers are one governmental response to information overload. They provide a mechanism for dealing with a large quantity of complex scientific and technical information. In spite of their value to federal agencies, however, some critics have charged that they are redundant. In addition, when the IACs make information available to the general public, other major issues concerning pricing of information, marketing of services and role identity arise.

Other Information Services

There are numerous other information systems in operation within the federal government. Descriptions presented here are meant to be illustrative rather than comprehensive. They serve to illustrate the breadth of efforts. Although the primary purpose of most of these systems is to facilitate internal information management, most of them also provide services to the public and to other libraries. It is in the context of information distribution and direct public services that the most controversial issues arise.

FEDERAL INFORMATION DISTRIBUTION

While the federal government must collect vast amounts of information to perform its myriad functions, it is also a formidable producer and distributor of information. Some researchers have estimated that the federal government spends over $15 billion annually on the production and distribution of information. That includes the writing, publication, storage, distribution and use of materials. Distribution of scientific and technical information alone accounts for annual federal expenditures of approximately $6.4 billion.[14]

The U.S. Government Printing Office (GPO) is the primary printer and distributor of documents originating in the federal government. It is governed by the Congressional Joint Committee on Printing (JCP) and distributes material through the Depository Library Program and the Sales Program. Although GPO is the principal distributor of federally produced information, other distribution systems abound. Members of Congress distribute materials free to constituents, individual agencies sell or give away their own publications and the National Technical Information Service sells a wide assortment of scientific and technical reports directly to the public.

Joint Committee on Printing

The Congressional Joint Committee on Printing (JCP) was created in 1846 to protect the federal government from corrupt printing practices. Its authority was expanded by the Printing Act of 1895, which established JCP as a permanent committee. At the same time, other laws regulating public printing and document distribution were revised, and the position of "public printer" responsible for the Government Printing Office was established.

The JCP is composed of the chairman and two members of the House Administration Committee and the chairman and two members of the Senate Rules Committee. The chairman of JCP is elected annually, and the position is usually passed back and forth between the House and the Senate.

The JCP acts as the Board of Directors of the Government Printing Office. It has broad authority under Title 44 of the United States Code to "use any measures it considers necessary to remedy neglect, delay, duplication, or waste in the public printing and binding and the distribution of government publications."

In exercising its authority, the JCP may conflict with directives of the Office of Management and Budget (OMB), especially in its administration of the Paperwork Reduction Act. JCP may also conflict with the activities of private companies that wish to print and distribute government publications for profit.

Government Printing Office/Depository Library Program

The Government Printing Office was established by Congress in 1860. In addition to printing and binding government documents, it prepares, catalogs, and distributes and sells government publications. In a single year, GPO distributes more than 20 million pieces of material representing 42,000 titles to depository libraries alone. In 1983 the number of depository libraries stood at 1373.

The Depository Library Program is administered by the Superintendent of Documents within the GPO, with oversight responsibility exercised by the Joint Committee on Printing. All of these activities are governed under Title 44 of the *United States Code.*

Since the 1970s, there have been repeated attempts to revise Title 44. Most of these revisions would remove GPO from legislative oversight, abolish the Joint Committee on Printing and establish GPO as an independent agency. Some suggested revisions would increase the role of the private sector as well. To date (1983), however, none of the proposed revisions have passed.

The Depository Library Program (DLP) began in 1813, when Congress decided that 200 copies of selected documents should be made available to each state and territorial government and to academic institutions and historical societies. The system through which depository libraries and other institutions are designated by senators and representatives was formalized by joint resolutions of Congress in 1857 and 1859. Although the depository program was initially assigned to the Department of the Interior, it was transferred to the Government Printing Office with passage of the 1895 Printing Act.

The most recent changes to the general scope and structure of the Depository Library System were initiated in 1962, with the passage of the Depository Library Act. The Act increased institutional designations of "depository library" from one to two per congressional member, established regional and selective depositories, required GPO to include non-GPO publications in the depository system, and allowed selective depositories to discard publications after five years with the permission of the governing regional depository.

Significantly, the legislation also required government agencies to furnish the Depository Library System with copies of any title that was not published through the GPO. The agencies were required to provide the copies at their own cost, and GPO was charged with distributing the copies throughout the Depository Library System. Prior to 1962 there had been a pronounced trend away from depository distribution. By 1960 there were some 350 agencies operating approved field printing plants, and officials estimated that 80% of federal agency printing was conducted through non-GPO and non-depository production.[15]

In the 15 years following the enactment of the Depository Library Act, GPO and the Depository Library System often failed to comply with the provision concerning distribution of non-GPO published documents. But in March of 1977, the Joint Committee on Printing approved GPO's request to convert these non-GPO materials to microfiche for depository library distribution. Since the microform program began in 1977, it has been expanded to include some GPO-produced documents as well. In its first three years (1977-1980), the microform program distributed over 47,000 titles and nearly 17 million pieces. In 1980 alone, the program distributed 24,930 titles and 8.2 million pieces.[16]

The ambitious microform program has been accompanied by stepped-up efforts to improve bibliographic control. Cataloging records are now entered into the OCLC computerized cooperative cataloging network, making it easier for users in all areas of the country to locate and borrow materials that are available through the depository system.

National Technical Information Service

Although GPO handles the bulk of general federal information distribution, the National Technical Information Service plays an enormously important role in the distribution of scientific and technical information, most of which is not published by GPO. The magnitude of the contribution made by NTIS can be seen in some statistics from FY 1977, a year in which GPO handled approximately 3800 research reports and sold a total of 3 million copies of those reports, while NTIS handled 85,000 research reports and sold approximately 4 million copies.[17]

Establishment and History

NTIS was officially established in 1970 by the Secretary of Commerce under Department Organization Order 30-7A. It traces its origins back almost 40 years, however, to the Publications Board that was formed in 1945 to collect and declassify World War II technical data for dissemination to industry. In 1946 the Department of Commerce consolidated the activities of the board and other organizations through the creation of the Office of Technical Services.

The functions of the Office of Technical Services were expanded by law in 1950, when the Department of Commerce was directed to set up and maintain a national clearinghouse for scientific and technical information. Functions were further expanded in 1964, when the Federal Council for Science and Technology recommended that the Office of Technical Services become the Clearinghouse for Federal Scientific and Technical Information.

With the reorganization of 1970, the Clearinghouse for Federal Scientific and Technical Information was abolished and its functions were transferred to NTIS. NTIS was charged with carrying out the provisions of Title 15 of the *United States Code*, the provisions that cover the maintenance of a clearinghouse for technical information. This statute requires NTIS to recover its costs from sales, and the service has become self-supporting.

Purpose

The purpose of NTIS is to collect reports produced or funded by federal, state and local governments containing scientific and technical information. It then provides private businesses, individuals, universities, federal agencies, state and local governments and international customers with access to the documents. NTIS is, quite simply, the central point in the United States for the public sale of government-funded research and development reports.

NTIS collects reports issued by the National Aeronautics and Space Administration, the Departments of Defense, Energy, Commerce, Health and Human Services and more than 300 other organizations. In 1980 NTIS added 77,000 new information items to its collection. The NTIS collection currently exceeds 1.2 million documents, of which 170,000 are of foreign origin. In 1980 it sold more than 6 million items to more than 100,000 customers, with total sales amounting to $21,800,000.

Distribution Services

To enhance its ability to distribute needed information and to ensure that it remains self-supporting, NTIS aggressively markets its services and is constantly developing new mechanisms to maintain better control of its collection. Some of these efforts include:

• Maintenance of an online computer search service (NTISearch) that contains abstracts of 650,000 federally sponsored research reports published since 1964;

• Lease on magnetic tape of the NTIS Bibliographic Data File that includes published and unpublished abstracts;

• Publication of a biweekly journal (*Government Reports Announcements and Index*) that contains abstracts of new research reports and other specialized technical information;

• Development and maintenance of a standing-order microfiche service (Selected Research in Microfiche, or SRIM) that automatically provides subscribers with the full texts of selected documents; and

• Publication of a newsletter containing information about government technology available for licensing (*Government Inventions for Licensing*).

NTIS has also been a leader in providing access to government-generated data banks and selected computer software. As part of a clearinghouse effort initiated in 1980, NTIS provides support to information vendors while refining data and programs to meet its own customers' needs.

Other new projects initiated within NTIS include: the creation of the Center for Utilization of Federal Technology (CUFT), which is charged with the improvement of the flow of knowledge from federal laboratories and R&D centers to the private sector; identification and acquisition of foreign technological information related to increasing productivity through a Foreign Technology Utilization project; and development of a new program concerning patent licensing and patent information conducted in cooperation with the Patent and Trademark Office.

The Future of NTIS

In spite of the extraordinary services provided by NTIS, its future is by no means secure. The Information Industry Association (IIA) claims that if NTIS were eliminated, "a void would be created that the private sector would fill."[18] Moreover, IIA feels that NTIS has a "chilling effect" on private sector information providers.

Clearly, the continued existence of NTIS will depend more on the resolution of some important policy issues than on any evaluation of NTIS performance. In a conservative political climate that favors private sector interests, NTIS finds itself facing a curious dilemma. If it fails to recover costs, it is likely to be shut down because it costs the federal government money. If it succeeds financially, it demonstrates that its activities could be handled profitably by the private sector.

ISSUES RAISED BY FEDERAL INFORMATION ACTIVITIES

Although the overall responsibility of the federal government to collect and distribute information has been recognized since the earliest days of the republic, recent political trends have brought the degree of federal commitment in this area into question. Clearly, the federal government must collect information for its own use. To this end, we have seen the growth and development of the national libraries, the federal libraries and numerous information systems and centers. While there have been some efforts in the early 1980s to revise Office of Management and Budget Circular A-76 to provide for private sector management of smaller federal libraries and information centers, most of the federal library policies continue unchallenged.

The more problematic issues arise from the federal government's information distribution activities. Some of the issues include: the appropriate role of the federal government as a producer and distributor of information, appropriate pricing of publications, possible elimination of redundancy of effort within the federal government itself, relationship between the public and private sectors in the distribution of government-produced information and tension between the principles of "freedom of information" and "privacy."

These issues involve social, political, economic and technological considerations. As a result, their resolution will rest on a complex combination of legislation, regulation and funding decisions. No matter how they are resolved in the short term, however, these issues are likely to recur as political and economic conditions change.

The primary political question to be addressed is not whether the federal government should collect, organize and use information for its own purposes, but to what extent and under what conditions it should distribute that information. Those issues are hotly debated and will be addressed in Chapter 6.

CONCLUSION

This chapter has examined the way in which the government manages its own information. It has considered the federal government as both a producer and consumer of information. Although these activities may not be as visible as library grants-in-aid or as vocal as federal policy development, they consume most of the federal dollars invested in information-related activities. Moreover, it can be argued that this investment is the most significant that the federal government makes in the general development of library and information services.

FOOTNOTES

1. Charles A. Goodrum, *The Library of Congress* (New York: Praeger, 1974).

2. *Ibid.*

3. Mark Hatfield, "Library of Congress," *Statesman* (Salem, OR: January 4, 1981).

4. Herbert Putnam, "What May Be Done for Libraries by the Nation," *Library Journal* 26:10-11 (January 1901).

5. Susan K. Martin, *Library Networks, 1981-1982* (White Plains, NY: Knowledge Industry Publications, Inc., 1981).

6. *Ibid.*

7. H.D. Avram and S.E. McCallum, "Directions in Library Networking," *Journal of the American Society for Information Science* 31:438-444 (November 1980).

8. *Ibid.*

9. Scott Adams, "Army Medical Library and Other Medical Libraries of the Nation," *College and Research Libraries* 9:126-132.

10. *United States Government Manual 1980-1981* (Washington, DC: Office of the Federal Register, 1980).

11. Robert B. Mehnert, "National Library of Medicine" in *The Bowker Annual of Library and Book Trade Information* (New York: Bowker, 1980).

12. "National Agricultural Library Overhaul Urged by Blue Ribbon Federal Panel," *Library Journal* 108:536 (March 15, 1983).

13. National Referral Center, *Directory of Federally Supported Information Analysis Centers* (Washington, DC: National Technical Information Service, 1974).

14. Donald W. King, "Scientific and Technical Information: Current Issues Concerning Government and this Essential National Resource." Discussion paper prepared for presentation to the Commerce Technical Advisory Board, January 6, 1981.

15. Bernard M. Fry, *Government Publications: Their Role in the National Program for Library and Information Services* (Washington, DC: National Commission on Libraries and Information Science, 1978).

16. *The ALA Yearbook 1981* (Chicago: American Library Association, 1981).

17. Donald W. King, op. cit.

18. Unpublished letter from Bob Willard, Information Industry Association, to Bernard Wunder, September 14, 1981.

4

Grants-in-Aid Programs

Grants-in-aid programs provide an especially important type of federal assistance to libraries. Beginning with the Library Services Act of 1956, which initially provided $2.1 million to aid rural public libraries, federal grants-in-aid programs to libraries grew to a combined funding high of $266 million in FY 1979. Nevertheless, aid to libraries has been exceedingly small compared to most other federal expenditures. Since the establishment of the three major library aid programs—the Library Services Act/Library Services and Construction Act, the Elementary and Secondary Education Act/Elementary and Secondary Education Consolidation and Improvement Act, and the Higher Education Act—the federal government has invested approximately $2.4 billion in libraries (see Table 4.1), a figure that amounts to less than one fifth of the proposed expenditures on the MX missile.

In another comparison, the Urban Library Council has demonstrated that support for libraries is minimal compared to other federal programs.[1] ULC notes that the federal income taxes paid by a typical family of four earning $20,000 per year go to support programs as follows:

Military	$606.43
Debt service	346.43
Education	62.43
Highways	43.43
Food stamps	38.43
Housing	28.43
Price supports	21.43
IRS	19.43
Postal subsidy	11.43
Congress	6.43
Amtrak	4.43
Public libraries	.43

Table 4.1 Summary of Federal Library Appropriations, Fiscal Years 1956-1983 (in millions)

Program	1956-75 (total)	1976	1977	1978	1979	1980	1981	1982	1983	Total
Library Services and Construction Act										
Title I (Public Library Services)	$485.4	$61.4	$56.9	$56.9	$62.5	$62.5	$62.5	$60.0	$60.0	$968.1
Title II (Public Library Construction)	174.1[1]	0	0	0	0	0	0	0	0	174.1
Title III (Interlibrary Cooperation)	24.3[2]	3.2	3.3	3.3	5.0	5.0	12.0	11.5	11.5	79.1
Elementary and Secondary Education Act										
Title IV-B (Consolidated Program)	NA[3]	68.7[6]	154.3[6]	167.5[6]	180.0[7]	171.0[7]	171.0[7]	NA[8]	NA[8]	912.5[9]
Higher Education Act										
Title II-A (Resources)	145.5[4]	9.9	9.9	9.9	10.0	5.0	3.0	1.9	1.9	197.0
Title II-B (Demonstration)	21.4[2]	1.0	1.0	1.0	1.0	.3	.5	.4	.2	26.8
Title II-B (Training)	39.6[4]	.5	2.0	2.0	2.0	.7	.7	.4	.6	48.5
Title II-C (Research)	Did not exist until 1978			5.0	6.0	6.0	6.0	5.7	6.0	34.7
TOTAL	$890.3[5]	$144.7	$227.4	$245.6	$266.5	$250.5	$255.7	$79.9[10]	$80.2[10]	$2440.8[9]

[1]1965-73.
[2]1967-75.
[3]ESEA Title II, 1967-75, school library resources.
[4]1966-75.
[5]Funds for ESEA 1966-75 (then Title II) not included.
[6]Appropriation is for the consolidation program: school library resources and textbooks; instructional equipment; and guidance, counseling, and testing.
[7]Appropriation estimate is for the revised consolidation program: school library resources and instructional equipment.
[8]Under the Education Consolidation and Improvement Act of 1981, school library resources and instructional equipment became one of 11 eligible categories for which states could allocate federal block grant funds.
[9]Does not include funds for ESEA 1966-75 or allocations made to school libraries under the ECIA block grant program.
[10]Does not include allocations made to libraries under the ECIA block grant program.

Sources: 1956-78-OLLR FY Budget Justification Document cited in National Commission on Libraries and Information Science, "Prospects, Possibilities and Alternatives for Federal Support of Libraries and Information Services: Design for the 1980s," a background paper, revised October 1978, Washington, DC, 1978, p. 24.
1979-ALA Washington Newsletter, Vol. 30, No. 1, Washington, DC, American Library Associaton, January 29, 1979.
1980-ALA Washington Newsletter, Vol. 31, No. 10, Washington, DC, American Library Association, August 7, 1979.
1981-ALA Washington Newsletter, Vol. 32, No. 1, Washington, DC, American Library Association, February 10, 1981.
1982-ALA Washington Newsletter, Vol. 33, No. 14, Washington, DC, American Library Association, December 31, 1982.
1983-Library Programs Division, Department of Education (telephone conversation).

Total federal outlays for library support in FY 1975 amounted to $161 million, a figure representing 0.3% of all federal grants-in-aid.[2] In the same fiscal year, only 5% of total public library support was derived from federal sources, while 12.9% came from state governments. Local governments continued to carry the bulk of the responsibility by providing 82.1% of public library support.

In spite of the relative meagerness of the funds, however, federal grants have had a major impact on libraries. They have provided incentives for the development of specific types of services and have encouraged important nationwide initiatives. This chapter will explore how the federal system of library grants developed and how each of the major formula grant programs operates. Discretionary grants (federal grants awarded on a competitive basis to support individual library projects) are described in Chapter 5.

Formula grants are made available to all libraries that meet certain conditions. The principal legislative acts that provide this type of support for libraries are the Library Services and Construction Act (LSCA), the Elementary and Secondary Education Act (ESEA), and the Higher Education Act (HEA). All of these programs are administered by the Library Programs Division (formerly the Office of Libraries and Learning Technologies) in the U.S. Department of Education.

THE DEVELOPMENT OF PUBLIC LIBRARIES

Grants-in-aid programs for libraries are comparatively new in library development. To understand their impact, it is important to note that grants-in-aid appeared at a time when the federal government was beginning to assume a broader support role and when libraries themselves (especially public libraries) were changing their own roles and responsibilities.

Public libraries have not always been public, at least not in the contemporary sense. A brief review of public library history, focusing on methods of funding and support, reveals recurring themes that have a direct bearing on the federal role today. These themes concern the relationship between library development and the federal government and the nature and purpose of library services. As a result, they have important implications for the federal role in supporting all types of libraries: public, elementary and secondary school, college and university, and others.

The Early Days*

The first public libraries in this country were public in the same way that a corporation is public; that is, they were not private or exclusive. Any individual could pay for a membership or buy shares in the library. Books were owned jointly and bought only for the use of members. Called subscription or social libraries, they were voluntary associa-

---

*The author is indebted to the following texts for information and ideas included in this section: George Bobinski, *Carnegie Libraries*; Sidney Ditzion, *Arsenals of a Democratic Culture*; Oliver Garceau, *The Public Library in the Political Process*; Michael Harris, *The Role of the Public Library in American Life*; and Jesse Shera, *Foundations of the Public Library*. Full citations for each of these texts are listed in the bibliography.

tions of individuals who wanted access to more books than any one member could afford to buy alone.

Some examples of this type of public library are the Philadelphia Library Company, founded by Benjamin Franklin in 1731, and the Boston Library, begun in 1792 through the sale of shares at $25 and annual subscriptions at $3. In some instances, the collections of subscription libraries were augmented by donations from private individuals. Thus, these early precursers to the public library were supported both by members' fees and philanthropy, and they were severely restricted in size, scope and use. Nevertheless, they flourished in the early days of the republic. By 1850 over 1000 such libraries were established in New England alone.

The Boston Model

In the second half of the 19th century, public libraries as we now know them began to appear. These libraries were established through local legislation, supported by taxation or voluntary gifts, and made available to every citizen of the town or city in which they were located. Using this definition, most library historians believe that the first public library was founded in 1833 in Peterborough, NH. The beginning of the public library movement, however, is usually pegged to the opening of the reading room of the Boston Public Library at the Adams House in 1854.

The opening of the reading room culminated several years of effort by a number of people, the most prominent of whom were Edward Everett, a former president of Harvard College and senator from Massachusetts, and George Ticknor, a professor of foreign languages at Harvard and leader of the Boston "Brahmins." While there is some disagreement about their motivation in establishing a free public library, many historians feel that it was based on their beliefs that adults are capable of unlimited self-improvement, that books are the primary means of education, and that most adults cannot afford to buy the books they need for continuing education.

Revisionist historians have made much of the conservative elitism of both Everett and Ticknor. They claim that Everett and Ticknor hoped to found an institution that would provide the common man with a means of improving himself, while at the same time contributing to the maintenance of the social order. Under this theory, theirs was not a love for the common man, but a fear of him. Whether we believe that Everett and Ticknor were motivated by liberal humanitarianism or conservative elitism, it is clear that the Boston Public Library came into existence not because the public demanded it, but because a few influential citizens felt that it was desirable.

Replication of the Boston Model

In the second half of the 19th century, America witnessed widespread replication of the Boston experiment. Historians cite several reasons for the rapid growth of libraries based on the Boston model: the increasing economic ability of many communities to support libraries; growing interest in scholarship and historical research; local pride and a stronger sense of social responsibility; the rise of an urban and industrialized population; a recognition of the social importance of universal public education; increased interest in individual self-improvement; and the interest and involvement of churches and religious groups. These trends, combined with the growing recognition of the role libraries could play in maintaining an informed citizenry, led to the establishment of 188 public libraries in 11 states between 1850 and 1875. In addition, by 1875 each state had established a state library for use by government officials, the judiciary and residents of the state capitol.

Growth and Development

During the last quarter of the 19th century, the public library also began to expand its services. Recreational reading and reference were added to the library's existing functions, and service to children was initiated. The thinking behind these innovations was reasonably straightforward. If the public library was to aid in educating and improving the masses, it was essential that all citizens be enticed into using the library.

During the late 19th and early 20th centuries, the influx of immigrants from eastern and southern Europe, Russia and China provided a new audience for the libraries' expanded services. Once again the libraries were perceived as playing a stabilizing, uplifting role. By helping immigrants learn the language and acquire knowledge of American culture, the library could assist with their amalgamation into the American mainstream.

Funding from Philanthropy

During this period, funding for libraries came largely from the philanthropy of wealthy citizens, most notably Andrew Carnegie. Their motivation was to provide "bootstrapping" opportunities for the aspiring poor. In addition, however, they viewed the library as a conservator of order and a monument to their own achievements. From 1886 to 1919, Carnegie alone provided over $40 million for the construction of 1679 library buildings in 1412 communities.

While no one can deny the positive economic aspects of this massive giving, there are other, more ambiguous effects that remain with us to this day. First, the nature of the giving emphasized the authoritarian nature of the public library. In many instances, the gifts came with conditions requiring the libraries to reflect the philosophy of the giver in their collections and services. Second, philanthropy by its very nature is independent of public desire. It is something imposed on society, rather than an expression of group action or wishes. Third, even the stipulation, not uniformly required or enforced, that individual communities must themselves contribute 10% of their Carnegie grant allocations to support of the library had questionable ramifications. Although there was no way of knowing at the time, many now feel that small communities simply do not have the economic base to operate a successful public library, and that the great number of libraries constructed in small communities has made the development of larger service areas more difficult. Even today over 40% of all public libraries serve localities with less than 3000 people. Nevertheless, spurred by big philanthropy, the number of public libraries had grown to 3873 by 1923, and they served approximately 53.5% of the entire U.S. population.

The Depression Era

Pushed by budget cuts during the depression of the 1930s, public libraries entered a period of reappraisal. Studies showing that 70% to 80% of public library borrowing in the 1920s and 1930s was for fiction books suggested that libraries were not providing the "social uplift" function that had long been considered one of their primary roles. Still, forced to choose between educational and recreational services, librarians chose to emphasize their educational role by curtailing branch library service, children's services and the purchase of fiction material.

The key questions of the period centered around library function, library funding and the relationship of the library to government. They were summarized most succinctly by Carleton B. Joeckel:

> Is free public library service really a proper and necessary function of government? . . . The second question will probably be: Has the public library a real platform—a definition of its purpose and of its vital necessity so brief and so simple that it will appeal to citizen and administrator alike? . . . Next, there is the eternal question of finance . . . Finally, the political scientist . . . [asks] just where does the library belong in the structure of local, county, or state government? . . . The traditional desire of the librarian for independence from the rest of government . . . will not meet with much sympathy from the student of government . . . Is it not somewhat curious that the public library, a democratic institution if there ever was one, should seem so fearful of democracy in its legally constituted form?[3]

The Public Library Inquiry of 1947-1950

These questions lingered, and they were addressed along with others in what is probably the most impressive study of public libraries to date. Funded by the Carnegie Corporation and conducted by the Social Research Council, *The Public Library Inquiry of 1947-1950* was a $200,000 survey and analysis of the American public library as a social institution. The results were published in seven volumes, several of which are still considered the most authoritative in their areas: *The Information Film, The Book Industry, Government Publications for the Citizen, The Public Library and the Political Process, The Public Librarian, The Library's Public* and the general report, *The Public Library in the United States.*

In summarizing the findings of the inquiry, Robert Leigh concluded that the public library was virtually a failure as a popular institution.[4] He noted that only 10% of an average community actively used the public library, and that library users were drawn primarily from the better educated segment of the population. Although Leigh believed that public libraries would be well advised to cater to this "natural audience," others drew different conclusions. Edward Bernays, for instance, found that the study had "created awareness both among librarians and laymen that the library occupies an extremely important place in the American pattern. The volumes of this survey have also made us realize that the library is in a position where its future is dependent upon public trends, attitudes and actions.''[5]

Changing Role and Services

As a result of the inquiry and a growing dependence on public support, libraries began once more to expand their services and improve the quality of services provided. While emphasis was still on the library's educational role, reference services began to expand and to play a larger part in the total library picture.

The growth of reference services was partly a reflection of an emerging role definition and partly a response to the need to attract public support. As a result of book burnings and other attempts to control information during World War II, there was a growing awareness of the importance of free access to information. This concept was quickly adopted as an essential element in the working of a democratic form of government, and libraries became the institutional representation of that ideal.

Increasingly, librarians spoke of the need for a neutral source of information on social, political and economic issues. Under this view, it was the responsibility of the librarian to make information on all sides of an issue available without bias. This approach was in tune with the times and, because it limited the library's editorial and gatekeeper functions, it was more in keeping with the library's proper role as a government-funded institution.

EARLY LOBBYING EFFORTS FOR FEDERAL FUNDING

Through the first half of the century, the American Library Association (ALA) waged a continuing crusade to involve the federal government in the support of libraries. ALA first lobbied for federal support in 1919 and 1920, but it intensified its lobbying efforts in the 1930s. In 1931 ALA proposed that Congress appropriate $1 million to be distributed to states according to their rural population over a 10-year period. This would equalize and encourage state expenditures for rural public library service. ALA also proposed the establishment of a federal library commission to administer the state programs.[6]

In 1935 and 1936, additional proposals attached to education bills called for federal aid to all types of libraries. Although none of the proposals passed, the lobbying effort proved to be the beginning of a long-term working relationship between ALA and the National Education Association, a relationship that continues today.

The one legislative success of the decade was the establishment in 1938 of the Library Services Division within the Office of Education. Over the objections of the U.S. Bureau of the Budget, an appropriation of $25,000 was passed to support this new division during its first year.[7]

After World War II, ALA continued its efforts to obtain federal grants for libraries.

Although the new ALA proposals were more limited in scope and unattached to education legislation, they still failed to pass.

In 1944 Carleton Joeckel, still committed to achieving federal aid for libraries, summarized the conclusions of a library institute sponsored by the University of Chicago that dealt with the subject. In a remarkably farsighted presentation, he called for "a system of not more than 1,000 strong public library units across the country, effective state library agencies with sufficient state aid to ensure a basic library program, and federal grants-in-aid to guarantee a minimum level of library services."[8] That same year, ALA voted to establish a Washington office.

FEDERAL AID TO PUBLIC LIBRARIES

Library Services Act

In 1956 the enactment of the Library Services Act (LSA) brought the federal government into the picture for the first time. This legislation was designed to assist in the establishment of library service in those areas previously unserved, especially in the rural parts of the country. In the same year, the Public Library Association's Coordinating Committee on Revision of the Public Library Standards issued new standards that differed significantly from earlier versions. The major difference was the introduction of a new organizational concept, the "system."

> Libraries are, therefore, urged to band together formally or informally in groups called 'systems.' In such systems large and small libraries in natural areas work together to make a wide range of library materials and services readily available to all residents. The systems in turn reach out to a wider world, drawing on even greater and more specialized resources offered by state and federal agencies. In a well-organized structure of library service, the reader in smaller and more remote places will have access not only to all books and materials in his region, but beyond that to the resources of the state and nation. Qualitative measures are emphasized based on the concept of library systems. A system contains a minimum of 100,000 population.[9]

While a causal connection cannot be proved, it is surely more than a coincidence that the need to establish access to materials outside of a single jurisdiction was articulated at the same time that requests for federal funds were being approved. It was also the age of the "baby boom," and increasing amounts of money at every level of government were being spent in support of education.

Although the timing of LSA coincided with these national trends, it was also the result of the 35 years of concerted effort on the part of ALA. Yet, in government at all levels, timing is often critical. By the time Congress came around to passing the Library Services Act, repeated surveys had revealed a shocking pattern of inadequate library service, especially in rural areas. For example, a study conducted by the U.S. Office of Education in 1956 indicated that 26 million rural residents were without any public library service, and that an additional 50 million had only inadequate service.[10]

Role of States

The Library Services Act was passed to deal quite specifically with the rural service problem. Its purpose was "to promote the further extension by the several states of public library services to rural areas without such service or with inadequate services."[11] In addition, it was seen by both Congress and ALA as only a temporary program to stimulate library support by the states. As he signed LSA into law, President Eisenhower reflected this understanding in his declaration that the act showed "promise of leading to a significant enrichment of the lives of millions of Americans, which I am confident will be continued by the states when this limited program comes to an end."[12] Significantly, LSA required that each state submit a plan for library development before it was eligible to receive a federal grant.

Influence of LSA

In 1960 LSA was extended for five more years with no significant change in the nature of the program. The LSA era was a good one for libraries, reflecting in many ways a stable and expanding economy, a national commitment to education and a sense of expansiveness. Most observers agree that LSA did much to expand library service to those previously without service, but its most significant contribution may have been its impact on funding sources. From 1939 to 1956, 87.3% of public library revenue was derived from local government, while 2.7% came from the state and 5.7% from other sources.[13] By 1964 only 82% was from local government, and the state contribution had grown to 8.4% of the total, for an increase of 5.7%.[14] This occurred with a federal investment of only $2 million-$7 million per year.

From another perspective, however, libraries did not do quite so well. Local governments continued to be the primary source of support for public libraries, and a quiet and subtle erosion of local funding had begun. According to one study, a comparison of library support in the 43 largest cities for the years 1959 and 1963-1964 revealed that "library support had increased 34.16% but the city operating budget was up 40.9%. The percentage of total local funds used for library purposes declined from 2.31% to 2.20%, representing a drop of 5% in 5 years."[15]

Library Services and Construction Act

To some extent, the slack was taken up by increased federal spending. In 1964, riding the tidal wave of federal support for "Great Society" ventures, the Library Services and Construction Act was enacted to replace the Library Services Act. LSCA differed from the preceding legislation in several significant ways. The scope was broadened to include funds for the construction and remodeling of library facilities, and the word "rural" was dropped, thereby making all public libraries eligible for assistance. In addition, to receive its full share of the federal appropriation, each state was required to provide matching state and local funds and to prepare a comprehensive plan for library development.

In subsequent years, LSCA has been amended to include federal support for: public library construction; the strengthening of urban libraries and state library agencies; the promotion of interlibrary cooperation; and the improvement of library services for physically handicapped, institutionalized, disadvantaged, bilingual and older persons.

At present, LSCA includes four authorized titles:

- Title I, Public Library Services;
- Title II, Public Library Construction;
- Title III, Interlibrary Cooperation; and
- Title IV, Older Readers Services.

General provisions of the legislation specify that a basic allotment is made to each sate for each title. Any funds remaining are distributed in proportion to the population of the state relative to the total U.S. population. Titles I and II also stipulate that the states and communities must match the federal contribution on the basis of a ratio of the state's per-capita income to the average per-capita income of the United States, but in no case is the federal share to be less than 33% or more than 66% of the cost of each program. The federal share for Titles II and IV is 100% (presuming, of course, that federal funds have been allocated for these titles).

Requirements for state participation in any LSCA program include: development of a basic state plan approved by the secretary of education; submission of a long-range plan that includes a five-year outline of state priorities, procedures and activities for meeting the library and information needs of the public; preparation of a program outlining the projects to be achieved for each title in which a state participates; and the provision of nonfederal matching funds for administration of the programs.

Title I, Services

Title I is the most general and comprehensive of the LSCA Titles. Title I funds may be used for books and other library materials, equipment and salaries, and other operating expenses. Title I funds can also be used for statewide planning and evaluation of programs, and for administration of the state plan.

To participate, individual states, Puerto Rico and the District of Columbia must meet minimum qualifications for the basic federal allotments of $200,000. American Samoa, Guam, the Virgin Islands and the Trust Territory of the Pacific Islands are eligible for a basic allotment of $40,000.

The purpose of Title I grants is to assist the states to:

1. Develop and improve public library service in geographical areas and to groups of persons without such service or with inadequate service;
2. Provide library services for:
   a. patients and inmates of state-supported institutions,
   b. the physically handicapped,
   c. disadvantaged persons in low-income areas, both urban and rural,
   d. persons of limited English-speaking ability;

3. Strengthen metropolitan public libraries which function as regional or national resource centers;
4. Strengthen the capacity of the state library agency to meet the library and information needs of all the people; and
5. Support and expand library services of major urban resource libraries which, because of the value of the collections of such libraries to individual users and to other libraries, need special assistance to furnish services at a level required to meet the demands made for such services.[16]

When appropriations for LSCA Title I exceed $60 million, a portion of the excess is earmarked for "major urban resource libraries." These funds are reserved by the legislation to libraries in cities having a population of 100,000 or more. The specific percentage of Title I funds above $60 million to be reserved for urban libraries in each state is based on its urban population in relation to total state population. However, no more than 50% of a state's share of appropriations above $60 million can be allocated to major urban resource libraries. In the 10 states having no city of 100,000 or more, these provisions do not apply.* These states may use all Title I funds for any of the Title I purposes. Since appropriations have rarely gone above $60 million, states have not had much experience with these provisions.

Title II, Construction

Although Title II had not been funded since 1973, a provision attached to a 1983 jobs bill signed by President Reagan authorized $50 million for library construction. Targeted for high-unemployment areas, the funding will be administered under LSCA Title II.

When available, Title II grants are made to states for the construction of new public library buildings and the acquisition, expansion, remodeling and alteration of existing buildings for use as public libraries. They may also be used for acquiring initial equipment of such buildings (books are excluded) and for architects' fees and the cost of acquiring land. As initially designed, the basic allotment for each state is $100,000, and the allotment for each outlying territory is $20,000. Construction or remodeling projects to remove architectural barriers and to reduce energy consumption are also eligible for support under Title II.

Title III, Interlibrary Cooperation

Title III was added by the LSCA Amendments of 1966. It provides grants to states for the planning, establishment and maintenance of cooperative networks of libraries at the local, regional or interstate level. These networks are to provide for "the systematic and effective coordination of the resources of school, public, academic and special libraries and information centers for improved supplementary services for special clientele served by each type of library or center." When appropriations are available, the basic allotment is $40,000 for each state and $10,000 for each outlying territory.

---

*According to the 1980 census, these states are: Delaware, Maine, Montana, New Hampshire, North Dakota, South Carolina, South Dakota, Vermont, West Virginia and Wyoming.

Title IV, Older Readers Services

Added by the Older Americans Amendments of 1973, Title IV has never been funded. Its purpose is to assist the states to provide library services for the elderly, including the purchase of special library materials; to pay salaries for elderly persons who wish to work in libraries; to provide in-home visits by library personnel to the elderly; and to furnish transportation to enable the elderly to have access to library services. The basic allotments are $40,000 for each state and $10,000 for each outlying territory.

PATTERNS OF PUBLIC LIBRARY FUNDING

Federal funding for public libraries has not followed a steady or regular growth path. In 1957 LSA received an initial appropriation of $2.1 million. By FY 1968, under the new Library Services and Construction Act, federal appropriations had increased to $40.9 million. By FY 1981, despite high inflation rates through much of the 1970s, appropriations under LSCA had grown to only $74.5 million. In late 1982, Congress voted to continue LSCA through FY 1983 at the FY 1982 funding level of $71.5 million.

These fluctuations in total federal appropriations have been accompanied by shifts in the funding allocated to individual library title programs. As mentioned earlier, LSCA Title IV (older readers services) was never funded. Funding for facilities construction under LSCA Title II was abandoned in 1973, and funding for Titles I and II has varied widely in response to the general state of the economy and the changing moods of Congress and the president. In FY 1982 appropriations for Title I (public library services) stood at $60 million, down $1.4 million from the FY 1976 appropriation. In contrast, funding for Title III (interlibrary cooperation) increased from $3.2 million in 1976 to $11.5 million in 1982. (See Table 4.1.)

Although LSA and LSCA have had a significant impact on public libraries, the fluctuations and uncertainty in federal appropriations have lessened their influence. Joseph Shubert has summarized some of the problems that libraries have faced during the LSA/LSCA years:

> As one examines the accomplishments and strengths as well as the weaknesses and problems of the LSA/LSCA years, one notices first the disparity between the promise and the reality of the program, i.e., the gap between legislative authorization and appropriation. For more than half of the LSCA program's history, and despite work on long-range planning, this gap, fiscal uncertainty, and delayed appropriations have necessitated ad hoc decisions for both state agencies and local libraries. Difficult decisions had to be made to keep programs afloat and staff together in "lean periods."[17]

Role of the Executive Branch

Much of the uncertainty over federal support for public library services can be traced to the differing attitudes of individual presidents and their administrations. From a peak during the Kennedy administration, support for libraries has experienced a steady decline.

Although much of the major library legislation was enacted during the Johnson administration, President Johnson expressed concern over the fragmentation of federal library programs, and John Gardner, his Secretary of Health, Education and Welfare, testified to Congress against expansion of LSCA. President Nixon proposed reductions in federal library support, supported general revenue sharing to replace categorical grants, and impounded library appropriations. Even President Carter, a strong library supporter, proposed lower levels of federal library support.

Most recently, President Reagan has recommended limitations on all non-defense spending, and authorizations for library programs have been among those experiencing reduced ceilings and impoundments. In addition, the Reagan administration has displayed renewed enthusiasm for grant consolidation and the establishment of block grants (a subject that will be discussed in more detail in the section on aid to elementary and secondary school libraries).

Evaluation and Conclusions

One concern about LSCA has been the extent to which federal funds are actually used to underwrite local public library services. An evaluation of LSCA Title I published in 1981 found that public libraries spent 43.3% of these monies in FY 1975, with state agencies consuming 28.9% and regional public libraries spending 20.7%. In FY 1978, however, usage patterns changed. Local public libraries spent only 35.2% of Title I funds, while state agencies increased their share to 35.2%.[18]

In another evaluation of LSCA, the researchers concluded:

> . . . as a fiscal subsidy method, the LSCA provisions represent a rather crude mechanism utilizing factors more appropriate in a tax redistribution scheme than a goal oriented aid system. The total cost . . . seems to be an expensive underwriting of the status-quo in a functional area where directed expansion and development are needed. It is difficult to achieve planned objectives under this kind of arrangement.[19]

As these evaluations and observations suggest, the Library Services and Construction Act is far from perfect. Funding has been uneven and unpredictable, making planning awkward and uncertain. LSCA has, however, contributed much to library development and cooperation. It has provided incentive for state participation in library development, and has thereby stimulated resource-sharing activities at the state and local level. It has contributed directly to network development and operation through Title III, and it has encouraged libraries to seek cooperative solutions to common problems through Title I. The ubiquitous nature of LSCA funding, its requirement that state and local governments provide matching funds, and its strengthening of state library agencies have been key ingredients in the growth of libraries.

AID TO ELEMENTARY AND SECONDARY SCHOOL LIBRARIES

In the mid-1960s, at the height of the "Great Society" era, the American Library Association successfully lobbied for federal legislation to aid libraries in elementary schools, secondary schools and institutions of higher learning. ALA's efforts resulted in two major pieces of legislation: the Elementary and Secondary Education Act of 1965 (ESEA) and the Higher Education Act of 1965 (HEA). This section will analyze the scope and impact of ESEA. HEA will be discussed later in the chapter.

Elementary and Secondary Education Act of 1965

The largest of all the federal grants-in-aid programs for libraries, Title II of ESEA initially authorized $100 million for the development of public and private school libraries. It provided for the purchase of books, periodicals, audiovisual materials, textbooks and other instructional materials. Funds were allocated as outright grants with no matching requirements, and individual states were responsible for drafting plans to distribute their allocations to public, private and parochial schools.

Since its introduction in 1965, the ESEA grants-to-school libraries program has undergone a number of important changes. A major change occurred in 1974, when the Education Amendments Act placed the library portion of ESEA under Title IV-B (Consolidated Program). In addition to providing funds for library materials, Title IV-B included support for textbooks, instructional equipment, and guidance, counseling and testing services. Four years later, the Educational Amendments of 1978 extended ESEA through September 30, 1983 and removed guidance, counseling and testing from the consolidated grant program.

Education Consolidation and Improvement Act

Despite the extension, ESEA was superseded by the Education Consolidation and Improvement Act (ECIA) of 1981. This legislation, part of the Reagan administration's commitment to a reduced federal role, established a block grant system of federal education funding to states. States can use their block grants to support educational programs and purchases that fall within 11 eligible categories, one of which is the acquisition of school library resources and instructional equipment. The 11 eligible categories replace 33 existing federal education programs. One goal of the block grant approach is to reduce federal education funding (the funding previously allocated to the 33 programs) by 20%.

In addition to reducing funding, ECIA eliminates almost all federal requirements for distributing the block grant allocations. As a result, there is no assurance that states and local school systems will maintain existing levels of support for school libraries. (See Figure 4.1.)

Comparison of ESEA and ECIA

While the legislation seems guaranteed to generate heated competition among programs for a decreasing amount of funds, a real evaluation is impossible until the ECIA program has been in operation for several years. Still, a comparison of ESEA, Title IV-B and ECIA, Chapter 2 reveals a number of likely trouble spots. (See Figure 4.1.)

As Figure 4.1 shows, the shift from ESEA categorical grants to ECIA block grants clearly represents a major change in the fortunes of school libraries. Without a major change in political philosophy, there is likely to be a significantly smaller funding pie and many more groups reaching for a piece.

Funding Patterns Under ESEA

Even under previous legislation, however, the fortunes of school library grant programs did not always run smoothly. As with LSCA, there have always been discrepancies between the promise and the payoff. As Table 4.2 indicates, the commitment to school library support was uncertain even before the advent of ECIA.

Influence on Libraries

In spite of the relatively small total investment and the volatility of the funding, school library aid programs have had an enormous impact on school library development. The *National Inventory of Library Needs—1975* indicates that in 1963-1964 only 56% of all schools, serving three fourths of the nation's elementary and secondary school students, had school library/media centers. By 1974, after eight years of school library aid totaling a little more than $500 million, five out of every six schools, serving 97.5% of U.S. public school students had a school library/media center.[20]

The survey also found that: "Library/media center service was in 1974 provided to 50% more school children—14.6 million more—than was the case in 1964. The number of school library/media centers has increased over the decade from 56,000 in schools of 150 pupils or more to an estimated total of 74,725. This achievement of extending service to essentially the entire public school population has been accompanied by moderate increases in resources."[21] While the study did not claim that these advances were the result of ESEA subsidy, one might surmise that some causal relationship is possible since the period of progress corresponds so directly to the period in which the school library aid programs were implemented. The total federal investment during the 10 year period was a little over one dollar per year per student.

AID TO ACADEMIC AND RESEARCH LIBRARIES

Although President Kennedy proposed aid for college and university libraries in his education message of 1963, a program of federal support for academic and research libraries was not actually funded until 1965, when Congress passed the Higher Education Act.

The suggestion that the federal government should provide support for large research libraries grew from a study of postsecondary education conducted by the Carnegie Corporation. In the study the Carnegie Corporation observed that large research libraries were suffering from growing demands on their collections and declining resources available to sustain and develop them. It concluded that a $10 million program of federal aid for research libraries was necessary. According to the study, the federal aid should be allocated on the basis of the number of doctoral degrees awarded and the amount of federal support of academic science in each institution.[22]

Figure 4.1 Comparison of ESEA Title IV-B and ECIA Chapter 2

ESEA TITLE IV-B	**ECIA CHAPTER 2**

Purpose

To provide assistance to local education agencies through grants to states for the acquisition of school library/media center resources and instructional equipment for public and private schools.

To provide resources to strengthen the ability of states and local schools to improve educational services.

Funding

This title is advance funded; that is, appropriations approved in one fiscal year are actually distributed in the following fiscal year. Appropriation for 1981 was $171 million.

Authorization is $565 million for FY 1982, $593.3 million for FY 1983, $622.9 million for FY 1984, $654.1 million for FY 1985, and $686.8 million for FY 1986. The appropriation for FY 1981 was $537.5 million and for FY 1982 $483.8 million.

Distribution

Appropriations are distributed to the states on the basis of the ratio of children in each state aged five to seventeen to the number of such children in all the states. The State educational agency may use 5% or $225,000, whichever is greater, for administrative purposes.

Ninety-five percent of the funds are to be distributed among local educational agencies on the basis of public and private school enrollments, but "higher per pupil allocations" are to be provided to schools in areas where poverty has limited the tax money available for education, where the local tax effort is higher than the state average but per pupil expenditure is still below average, and to schools in areas that have "the greatest numbers or percentages of children whose education imposes a higher than average cost per child, such as children from low-income families, children living in sparsely populated area, and children from families in which English is not the dominant language."

Services are to be provided to both public and private school children. Local educational agencies have complete discretion to determine how the IV-B funds they receive are to be apportioned among the various programs, provided the items acquired are to be used for instructional purposes only.

Appropriations are allotted to the states on a school-age population basis except that no state is to receive less than .6% of the total allotted. One percent of the total is reserved for insular areas and Indian reservations.

States may carry out Chapter 2 activities directly or through subgrants or contracts to local education agencies or nonprofit private organizations or institutions, including community-based organizations. There is no requirement to pass any funds through to the local level

States must prepare an annual plan and report on activities every two years. Both must be made public within the state, with opportunity for public comment, but there is no requirement for federal review of these documents. Local education agencies and other subgrantees must provide "such information as the State deems necessary" for preparation of the plan and report. No local plans are required for Chapter 2.

Figure 4.1 Comparison of ESEA Title IV-B and ECIA Chapter 2 (cont.)

ESEA TITLE IV-B	ECIA CHAPTER 2

Authorized Activities

Authorized activities are:

1. Acquisition of school library resources, textbooks, and other printed and published instructional materials for the use of children and teachers;

2. Acquisition of instructional equipment, and materials suitable for use in providing education in academic subjects, for use by children and teachers.

Authorized activities are:

1. Projects to strengthen the curriculum of schools, such as basic skills instruction, law-related education, and arts education;

2. Projects to increase community involvement in school programs;

3. Professional development programs for teachers, administrators and other school personnel;

4. Pilot and demonstration projects, including improving education for children with special educational needs, addressing problems such as student motivation and school violence, using technology to improve the quality of instruction and improving educational equity for women;

5. Regional & interstate educational programs;

6. Technical assistance and dissemination of information;

7. Studies and other projects to improve school management and the coordination of resources in a school to meet the needs of individual children;

8. The acquisition for instructional purposes of school library resources, textbooks and instructional equipment and materials;

9. To the extent necessary to implement other eligible activities, repairs and minor remodeling of schools and other instructional facilities;

10. Programs to strengthen state educational oversight and management through such activities as the collection and analysis of statistics, consultation and advice to local education agencies, studies of education policy issues and assessment of educational progress, and exchanging information about successful educational practices;

11. Administration activities, including planning, technical assistance, evaluation, information dissemination and audits.

Maintenance-of-Effort

There is a maintenance-of-effort provision that provides for maintaining state and local effort on either a per-student or an aggregate expenditure basis, and for waivers under special circumstances.

There is no requirement for maintenance-of-effort or for matching funds, and no prohibition against replacing state and local education funds with federal dollars.

Source: American Library Association, Washington, D.C., various publications.

Table 4.2 Authorization, Administration Requests, and Appropriations for School Library Aid Programs FY 1966-1981
(in thousands)

	Authorization	Request	Appropriation
ESEA II			
FY1966	$100	$100	$100
1967	125	105	102
1968	150	105	99
1969	162	46	50
1970	200	. . .	42
1971	200	80	80
1972	210	80	90
1973	220	90	100
1974	220	. . .	90
1975	220	90	95
ESEA IV-B			
(Consolidated Program)			
FY1976	such sums		$ 68
1977	such sums		154
1978	such sums	$154	167
1979	such sums	167	180
1980	such sums	149*	171
1981	such sums	. . .	171

*Reflects proposal to transfer $18 million to the new ESEA IV-D Guidance, Counseling, and Testing Program (formerly part of IV-B).

Source: R. Moltz, *Federal Policy and Library Support* (Cambridge, MA: MIT Press, 1976).

While the American Library Association agreed with the suggestion in principle, it felt that "research library" should be defined in a way that would include major urban public research libraries such as the New York Public Library. Congress concurred and, as a result, the Higher Education Act defined a "major research library" as:

> a public or private non-profit institution, including the library resources of an institution of higher education, an independent research library, or a State or other public library, having library collections which are available to qualified users and which (1) make a significant contribution to higher education and research; (2) are broadly based and are recognized as having national or international significance for scholarly research; (3) are of a unique nature, and contain material not widely available; and (4) are in substantial demand by researchers and scholars not connected with that institution.

Provisions of HEA

Originally, the Higher Education Act of 1965 contained three programs of interest to libraries:

• Title II-A provided funds for the acquisition of books, periodicals and other materials for college and university libraries;

• Title II-B provided support for library training and research and demonstration programs; and

• Title II-C supported a centralized cataloging and acquisitions program under the direction of the Library of Congress. (The Title II-C program was later shifted to the Library of Congress budget.)

In the Education Amendments of 1976, Congress added a new Title II-C to the Higher Education Act. Its purpose was to promote research and education of higher quality throughout the United States by providing financial assistance to major research libraries.

The Higher Education Act was further modified by the Education Amendments of 1980. As it exists today, HEA contains four sections that contribute to library development:

• Title II-A, College Library Resources;
• Title II-B, Library Training, Research and Development;
• Title II-C, Strengthening Research Libraries' Resources; and
• Title II-D, National Periodical System.

Title II-A, College Library Resources

Title II-A authorizes formula grants to elegible institutions of higher education for the primary purpose of acquiring books, periodicals, documents, magnetic tapes, phonograph records, audiovisual materials and other related library materials. With the passage of the Education Amendments of 1980, the purpose of this title was expanded to include "establishment and maintenance of networks for sharing library resources." The legislation provides for basic grants, called "resource development grants," of up to $10,000 for each institution. Under the 1980 amendments, supplemental grants that existed prior to 1980 were eliminated and special-purpose grants were moved to Title II-B.

The new version of HEA reflects the reality that since 1973 only basic grants have been funded. Because the appropriation level for Title II-A has been so low, these grants have provided very small amounts of funding ($5.0 million in FY 1980) to a great many institutions (2595 in FY 1980). As a result, the impact of Title II-A on library development has generally been minimal in the case of larger institutions and more significant in situations where smaller institutions were struggling to survive.

Total appropriations available under Title II-A have declined steadily since the late 1960s, when $25 million a year was provided for college library resources. By 1983 yearly appropriations had declined to slightly less than $2 million.

Title II-B, Library Training, Research and Development

Title II-B provides discretionary grants that are divided equally among a three-part program. This program consists of: library career training, research and demonstration grants, and special purpose grants. A discussion of these programs is included in Chapter 5.

Title II-C, Strengthening Research Libraries' Resources

In contrast to Title II-A, Title II-C provides large amounts of money to a relatively small number of institutions. Title II-C was enacted in recognition of the fact that major research libraries form the bibliographic foundation of our research resources, and that they require financial incentives to participate in resource-sharing activities with smaller libraries. Under Title II-C, grants are made to research libraries for the purposes of

> . . . maintaining and strengthening their collections, which are essential to scholarship and research on a national and worldwide basis, and to assist them in making their holdings available to individual researchers and scholars and to other libraries whose users have need for such research materials.[23]

Awards are made in three areas: 1) collection development, 2) preservation of materials, and 3) bibliographic control.

Estimates indicate that approximately 200 libraries currently fall within the definition of major research library. They include college and university libraries, public libraries, state libraries and private nonprofit research libraries. Up to 150 grants may be made annually, and regulations ensure equitable geographic distribution.

An analysis of Title II-C grants made in FY 1978, FY 1979 and FY 1980 suggests a definite trend toward increased support of networking activities. Table 4.3 shows the distribution of grants among the three program areas for the years listed above.

As Table 4.3 indicates, there is a clear and growing commitment to supporting activities that contribute to resource sharing through networking and bibliographic control. Although Title II-C is not generally thought of as a major source of financial support, it does provide some incentive for the larger libraries to participate in cooperative activities. In addition, unlike many other grants-in-aid programs, Title II-C has been able to maintain its initial level of funding. Appropriations for FY 1978, the first year of the program, were $5 million, and appropriations remained at or near the $6 million level through 1983.

Title II-D, National Periodical System

Title II-D was added to HEA in 1980. It has never been funded, and many feel that it will remain unfunded indefinitely, since it specifies that no money can be appropriated for

Table 4.3 Program Activity, Higher Education Act, Title II-C, 1978-1980

Year	Collection Development	Preservation	Bibliographic Control/Access
1978	$795,103	$1,340,554	$2,864,339
1979	628,443	1,393,201	3,978,366
1980	839,062	788,919	4,326,743
Total	$2,262,608	$3,522,674	$11,169,448

Source: Department of Education, Office of Libraries and Learning Technologies (now the Library Programs Division).

Title II-D until II-A, II-B and II-C are funded at FY 1979 levels. Under the legislation, Title II-D would establish a nonprofit National Periodical System Corporation to "assess the feasibility and advisability of a national system and, if feasible and advisable, design such a system to provide reliable and timely document delivery from a comprehensive collection of periodical literature." The legislation calls for the nonprofit corporation to be governed by a presidentially-appointed board representing all major interests, and for Congress to approve a design plan before the system is implemented.

Impact of HEA

The provisions of HEA reflect the realities of information needs and services in the academic world today. Through Title II-A grants, HEA contributes to the maintenance of a large number of academic libraries in colleges and universities of every size. On campuses throughout the country, these libraries make modest collections of frequently used materials available to both students and staff.

Title II-C, on the other hand, recognizes the national need to develop collections of significant size and scope. Through networking and interlibrary loans, these collections are then made available to students and researchers requiring materials that are in less frequent demand.

Both approaches are needed to ensure individual student development and the general growth of research knowledge. By supporting both the centralization of resources and their dissemination through local distribution outlets, HEA is in tune with the times and today's technological and economic imperatives.

AID TO MEDICAL LIBRARIES

The third piece of library legislation to pass in 1965 was the Medical Library Assistance Act (MLAA). Through this act, the Public Health Service was authorized to grant funds for the construction of medical libraries, training of librarians, expansion of medical library resources, and development of a national system of regional health science libraries under the National Library of Medicine.[24]

Under MLAA the National Library of Medicine administers grants for a variety of programs. These include: improving biomedical library resources; research in information sciences related to health; support of biomedical scientific publications; and training to integrate clinical practice, health research and education with appropriate computerized techniques.

Through its Regional Medical Library (RML) Program, NLM coordinates a nationwide network of 11 regional medical libraries and over 100 resource libraries. In addition, NLM supports library consortia comprised of cooperating health insitutions in large geographic areas. The entire regional medical library network generates an estimated 2 million interlibrary loan transactions each year.

The Medical Library Assistance Act enjoys the distinction of being the only library grants-in-aid program to receive continuing broad-based support. In FY 1974, a year in

Table 4.4 Expenditures for Library-Related Programs (in thousands)

Library-Related Programs	FY 1981 Appropriations	FY 1982 Reagan Budget	FY 1982 Continuing Resolution Appropriations	FY 1982 After Proposed Revisions	FY 1983 Authorization	FY 1983 Budget Allocations
Adult Education Act	$ 100,000	$ 84,480	$ 86,400*	$ 84,480	$ 100,000	—¹
Bilingual Education	161,427	126,553	138,057*	126,553	143,810	94,534
Corporation for Public Broadcasting	137,000	93,500	105,600*	105,600	130,000	85,000
ECIA Chapter 1 (ESEA I Disadvantaged Children)	2,951,692	2,358,240	2,739,449*	2,357,876	Formula based	1,942,000
Educating Handicapped Children (state grants)	874,500	672,436	931,008*	672,436	1,017,900	—²
HEA Title I-B, Education Outreach	2,200	—0—	—0—	—0—	8,000	—0—
III, Developing Institutions	120,000	129,600	124,416*	129,600	129,600	129,600
IV-C, College Work Study	550,000	484,000	528,000*	484,000	550,000	397,500
VI, International Education	19,800	14,960	19,200*	14,960	30,600	8,767
Indian Education Act	81,680	71,597	77,853	71,598	88,400	51,119
National Archives & Records Service	83,643	79,294	73,652*	73,652	44 USC 21-33	85,007
National Center for Educational Statistics	8,947	8,589	8,589*	8,589	8,947	8,747
National Endowment for the Arts	158,795	77,440	143,040	143,040	119,300	100,875
National Endowment for the Humanities	151,299	74,800	130,560	130,560	113,700 Needs new authorization	96,000
National Historical Publications & Records Commission	4,000	—0—	1,000*	1,000		286
National Institute of Education	65,614	53,389	53,389*	53,389	55,614	53,645
Postsecondary Education Improvement Fund	13,500	11,520	11,520*	11,520	13,500	11,900
Public Telecommunications Facilities	19,705	—0—	18,000*	18,000	15,000	—0—
Women's Education Equity	8,125	—0—	5,760*	—0—	6,000	—0—

*Funded only through 3/31/82 by a further continuing resolution, PL 97-92.
¹Included in block grant proposal for Vocational & Adult Education ($500 million budgeted).
²Included in block grant proposal for Special Education ($845.7 million budgeted).

Source: ALA *Washington Newsletter* Vol. 34, No. 14. (Washington, DC, American Library Association, February 19, 1982).

which all library aid programs were zero-funded by the Ford administration, the MLAA program received a 37% increase over the FY 1973 appropriation. In FY 1983, when the Reagan administration proposed the elimination of all library aid programs, aid to medical libraries stood out as the only exception to the proposed funding cuts. MLAA does require new authorization for FY 1984, however.

OTHER FEDERAL AID TO LIBRARIES

In addition to the specific library grants-in-aid programs described above, there are numerous other federal programs that have provided support for libraries. Some of those that have assisted libraries in the past include: the Higher Education Facilities Act, the Appalachian Regional Development Act, the Public Works and Economic Development Act, the Gifted and Talented Children Act and the National Foundation on the Arts and Humanities Act. Programs in existence in 1982 that may provide some assistance to libraries are listed in Table 4.4. Those programs that provide support for research and demonstration are discussed in Chapter 5.

CONCLUSION

Federal grants-in-aid to libraries are a relatively recent development in the history of libraries and in the history of the federal government. Not surprisingly, the passage of the Library Services Act in 1956 coincided with the introduction of the notion that libraries should form "systems" (larger units of service). Federal support for libraries expanded in the middle 1960s, with the introduction of legislation supporting school libraries, academic libraries and medical libraries. Appropriations swelled in the late 1960s as the country began to invest in social programs.

With the declining economy, the federal government appears to be abandoning its commitment to educational development. Unfortunately, this is happening at a time when libraries are growing increasingly interdependent, a trend that some analysts feel justifies the intervention of the federal government on a much broader scale.

There can be no doubt that the aid programs described above have justified their existence many times over. Repeatedly, an exceedingly small federal investment has provided the incentives needed for states and local communities to develop the capacity to provide needed library services. The primary question now is: Was the federal grants-in-aids program to libraries an historical anomaly reflecting a brief federal fling with social goals, or is there justification for a longer term federal involvement? This and other policy-related issues will be discussed in Chapter 6.

FOOTNOTES

1. *Urban Libraries Council,* flyer published and distributed by the Urban Libraries Council, Chicago, 1981.

2. Advisory Commission on Intergovernmental Relations, *Federal Involvement in Libraries* (Washington, DC: Advisory Commission on Intergovernmental Relations, 1980).

3. Carleton B. Joeckel, "Questions of a Political Scientist," *ALA Bulletin* 27:66-69.

4. Robert D. Leigh, *The Public Library in the United States* (New York: Columbia University Press, 1950).

5. Edward L. Bernays, "The Library Inquiry Is Not Over," *Wilson Library Bulletin* 25:245-246 (November 1950).

6. Dennis Thomison, *A History of the American Library Association: 1876-1972* (Chicago: American Library Association, 1978).

7. John M. Cohn, "The Impact of the Library Services and Construction Act on Library Development in New York State: A Study in Assessing the Effects of Federal Grants-in-Aid Legislation on the States." Dissertation, New York University, 1974.

8. Advisory Commission on Intergovernmental Relations, op. cit.

9. Public Library Association's Coordinating Committee on Revision of Public Library Standards, *Public Library Service: A Guide to Evaluation, with Minimum Standards* (Chicago: American Library Association, 1956).

10. James W. Fry, "LSA and LSCA, 1956-1973: A Legislative History," *Library Trends* 7-26 (July 1975).

11. P.L. 84-597, Sec. 2(a).

12. James W. Fry, op. cit.

13. Ann E. Prentice, *Public Library Finance* (Chicago: American Library Association, 1977).

14. *Ibid.*

15. *Ibid.*

16. American Library Association, Washington Office, *Library Services and Construction Act (LSCA)* (Washington, DC: American Library Association, 1979).

17. Joseph F. Shubert, "The Impact of the Federal Library Services and Construction Act," *Library Trends* 27-44 (July 1975).

18. Applied Management Sciences, Inc., *An Evaluation of Title I of the Library Services and Construction Act.* Final report prepared for Office of Program Evaluation, U.S. Department of Education (Washington, DC: U.S. Department of Education, 1981).

19. *Alternatives for Financing the Public Library: A Study Prepared for the National Commission on Libraries and Information Science* (Washington, DC: Government Printing Office, 1974).

20. Boyd Ladd, *National Inventory of Library Needs, 1975* (Washington, DC: National Commission on Libraries and Information Science, 1977).

21. *Ibid.*

22. Carnegie Council on Policy Studies in Higher Education, *The Federal Role in Postsecondary Education: Unfinished Business, 1975-1980* (San Francisco: Jossey-Bass, 1975).

23. *FY 80 Abstracts* (Washington, DC: U.S. Department of Education, Office of Libraries and Learning Technologies, 1980).

24. Robert J. Havlich, "Federal Assistance to Special Libraries" in "Federal Library Legislation, Programs, and Services," *ALA Bulletin* (February 1966).

5
Research and Demonstration

The United States currently spends approximately $60 billion for research and development, with about 47% of this funding provided by the federal government. Although the federal share is down from the 65% provided in the early 1960s, it represents the continuation of a long-term national commitment to the pursuit of knowledge. Since the late 1950s, most federal research funding has been allocated to defense and space programs. However, a significant amount has also gone to support research in science, medicine, education and other civilian areas.

The focus of federal support for research and development differs from that of industrial R&D funding, which usually goes to support programs that have a low risk and a high, short-term payoff. In contrast, federal R&D funding typically concentrates on programs that are of national concern, have little chance of producing direct financial benefits, carry a relatively high risk, or may take extended periods of time to produce useful results.

This chapter will begin by briefly reviewing the evolving responsibility of the federal government in providing support for research. It will then describe the need for and level of research conducted in the areas of library development, information services and information technology, both within the federal government and in the private sector. Finally, it will detail current research and demonstration support available from federal agencies concerned with library and information services.

BRIEF HISTORY OF FEDERAL INVOLVEMENT

Although the current federal investment in scientific research is significant, that has not always been the case. In 1940, prior to the U.S. entry into World War II, the annual amount allocated to research and development was only $75 million. By 1980 the federal investment in R&D had grown to more than $30 billion per year.

This dramatic shift in federal priorities reflects changes in the perceived roles of both the federal government and research itself. It was not until the Industrial Revolution that scientific and technological advancement was widely recognized as an important factor in the economic evolution of the country, and it was not until World War II that the impact of science and technology on national defense became generally apparent. During the war, the nation's leaders came to recognize that the federal government must begin making significant contributions to scientific and technological research if it hoped to continue fulfilling its obligations to ''promote the common defense'' and ''provide for the general welfare.''

Establishing a Federal Role

The modern era of federal involvement in research and development began during and immediately after World War II, when the government established a number of federal research centers. These centers included four Atomic Energy Commission (AEC) research laboratories, the Navy's Applied Physics Laboratories, the Navy's Center for Naval Analyses and its Ordnance Research Laboratory, the Air Force's RAND center, and the Army's Operation Research Office. But the big push for the federal government did not come until 1950, when the National Science Foundation was established to provide leadership and support for scientific research.

Through the 1950s, federal involvement in research continued to grow. During this period, the government agencies most heavily involved in research and development were AEC, the various Defense Department research agencies, the National Institutes of Health, the Department of Agriculture and the National Advisory Committee for Aeronautics. But the bulk of federal R&D funding went to military and weapons research. In FY 1956 the Department of Defense agencies alone accounted for 70% of federal research expenditures.

With the launching of the first earth satellite by the USSR in 1957, interest in space-related programs grew. As a result, defense and space programs combined to command over half of all funds devoted to research and development from 1957 to 1966, with that figure rising to 90% in the period from 1963 to 1966.

Recent Trends

As the urgency of the space program diminished in the 1970s, research programs began to broaden into areas outside of defense and space (although defense continued to account for the bulk of federal research expenditures). The overall role of the federal government during the 1970s can be seen by looking at the three separate areas of basic research, applied research and development. In 1973 the federal government was credited with financing 58% of total basic research, 24% of applied research, and 52% of all development.[1]

Growing concern over declining productivity in the United States has led some analysts to note that U.S. investment in research and development has been decreasing in recent years. As a percentage of gross national product, federal R&D funding declined from a high of 3% in 1964 to 2.3% in 1980. In contrast, the West German government increased its contribution from 1.6% in 1964 to 2.3% in 1980. In Japan the ratio grew from 1.5% in 1964 to 1.9% in 1980.[2]

While the United States percentage is still higher than that of most other nations, the U.S. government differs significantly in its use of research funds. In FY 1980 the government allocated 61% of its research and development funds to defense and space programs. In contrast, France, Japan and West Germany have tended to concentrate on research in the areas of economic development and the advancement of general knowledge. In the United States, the percentage of federal R&D funds allocated for national defense remained relatively constant at 47% to 50% from 1976 to 1980, while space-related R&D declined slightly to 14%. By 1980 civilian R&D projects accounted for 39% of federal research funds available. Of this, more than half was allocated to health and energy projects. General science projects received 3.9% of the total federal research funds available, while education and social service research drew 1.4%.[3]

LIBRARY AND INFORMATION SCIENCE RESEARCH

In the area of library and information science, the federal government spent approximately $58 million on research and development in the entire decade of the 1970s. In addition, the Council on Library Resources, Inc. contributed $5.3 million and the Carnegie Corporation of New York contributed $3.6 million.[4] This compares with $3.4 billion spent on research and development by the computer equipment industry during 1980 alone.[5]

Major Federal Agencies

Of the seven federal agencies that provide funding for library and information research, three agencies provide the major portion of support. In 1980 the total annual funding available from all seven was $6.4 million, down significantly from a 1975 high of $19.3 million. The seven agencies that fund library research, along with the total amount of funding each provided for library and information research from 1970 to 1980, are listed in Table 5.1.

Federal Activities in the 1970s

The research areas selected for funding from 1970 to 1980 reflected the growing importance of technology and the need for R&D in designing useful systems. According to *A Library and Information Science Research Agenda for the 1980s,* a report compiled for the Department of Education by Cuadra Associates, the three subject areas receiving the largest amounts of funding in the 1970s were: information retrieval system design and evaluation, management of library and information services and systems, and networking and resource sharing.[6]

But research grant programs are not the only way the federal government contributes to library research and development. As noted in Chapter 3, significant federal resources have been dedicated to the development of data bases at the Library of Congress, the Na-

Table 5.1 Funding Sources for Library and Information Research, 1970-1980 (in thousands)

Funding Agency	1970-71	1972-73	1974-75	1976	1977	1978	1979	1980	Total
National Science Foundation, Division of Information Science and Technology	NA	NA	$10,207	$4,237	$3,657	$4,576	$4,816	$5,570	$33,063
Department of Education/Office of Libraries and Learning Technologies/Library Research and Demonstration Branch	$2,347	$3,028	1,410	1,036	1,116	776	730	142	10,585
National Library of Medicine, Extramural Grants Program	1,659	842	2,091	604	803	932	268	NA	7,199
Council on Library Resources, Inc.	2,020	1,124	1,672	191	227	43	40	—0—	5,317
Carnegie Corporation of New York	—0—	1,423	404	11	515	406	635	194	3,588
National Endowment for the Humanities	50	—0—	1,803	452	35	57	262	16	2,675
National Library Service for the Blind and Physically Handicapped, Library of Congress	NA	NA	NA	180	301	—0—	955	284	1,720
Department of Education, National Institute for Education	—0—	—0—	450	—0—	130	75	442	—0—	1,097
National Commission on Libraries and Information Science	NA	204	292	49	—0—	88	—0—	136	769
TOTAL	$6,076	$6,621	$18,329	$6,760	$6,784	$6,953	$8,148	$6,342	$66,013

NA: Not Available.
*For multi-year awards, total dollar figures have been allocated to the year in which the award was made.
Source: *A Library and Information Science Research Agenda for the 1980s*, Santa Monica, CA: Cuadra Associates, 1982.

tional Library of Medicine and the National Agricultural Library. By developing the capacity to manage their own collections, these libraries have provided tools necessary for nationwide library development. The Library of Congress's development of MARC tapes is the most obvious example of the impact of federal internal research and development on libraries throughout the country.

Continuing Federal Role

Research and development, together with adequate funding and technology transfer, are critical elements in the growth of libraries. Arguing in support of continued federal funding, Miriam Drake has compared federal R&D funding for libraries to the subsidies provided to the airline and satellite industries, both of which were initially funded by the federal government.[7]

For several reasons, federal support for library R&D seems to make more sense now than ever. In most states and communities, tax revenue available for library support is declining. At the same time, recent technological developments have offered libraries a means of improving their productivity—a goal that is consistent with federal funding priorities. In addition, private sector R&D in information areas continues to be geared more toward immediate profit returns than long-term public concerns.

In many high technology industries, it is not unusual to find as much as 6% to 8% of net sales invested in research and development. Of this amount, the federal government may contribute as much as 50% of the total, and the figure is as high as 84% in the aircraft and missiles industries.[8]

Nevertheless, the amount of federal funding for information and library research has continued to decline. In the information industry, as defined rather restrictively by the Information Industry Association,* corporate investment in research and development was $146 million in 1979. Of those businesses reporting R&D expenditures, the average investment was 4% of net sales. During that same year, the federal government contributed $7.4 million to research and development in the whole area of library and information science. Based on these figures, the federal government invested only 4.8% of the total amount spent on R&D in the area of information services, an area that is growing rapidly and that offers potential solutions to national productivity problems.

DEPARTMENT OF EDUCATION, LIBRARY PROGRAMS DIVISION

Of all the federal funding agencies, the one that is by far the most significant in its impact on library development is the Library Programs Division (LPD). Formerly the Office of Libraries and Learning Technologies, LPD was renamed in 1983, when the division

---

*According to the Information Industry Association, information companies are "services which organize, manipulate, convert, deliver or communicate, process, analyze, impart information obtained from investigation, research, study or instruction."[9]

became part of the new Center for Education Improvement in the Department of Education. LPD is charged with administering the major federal library legislation, including the Library Services and Construction Act (LSCA) and the four library title programs funded through the Higher Education Act (HEA).

Most of the grants distributed through LPD are allocated on a categorical rather than discretionary basis. That is, a distribution formula is used, and funding is provided to all libraries and library agencies that qualify. Discretionary grants, on the other hand, are allocated to individual libraries and agencies on a competitive basis. The categorical grants available under LSCA and HEA were discussed in Chapter 4. This section will describe HEA Title II-B, the discretionary grant segment of HEA administered by LPD.

Provisions of Title II-B

As discussed in Chapter 4, HEA Title II-B was modified under the Education Amendments of 1980. Currently, Title II-B provides discretionary grants that are divided equally among a three part program: Library Career Training, Research and Demonstration, and Special Purpose Grants.

The Library Career Training Program provides grants for fellowships and traineeships (which must account for at least 50% of available monies), support for library institutes, and funding "to establish, develop, or expand programs of library and information science, including new techniques of information transfer and communication technology."

The Research and Demonstration Program provides grants "for research and demonstration projects related to the improvement of libraries, training in librarianship and information technology, and for the dissemination of information derived from such projects."

The Special Purpose Grants Program was transferred from Title II-A and expanded. In years that it is funded, this program provides grants to assist higher education institutions to meet special national or regional library or information science needs; establish and strengthen joint-use library facilities, resources or equipment; service their communities; and, with other library institutions, improve academic library services. Special purpose grants are not restricted to the acquisition of library materials. This program was not funded in FY 1983.

Funding Levels

Authorizations for HEA II-B were initially set at a heady $10 million for FY 1981, $30 million yearly for FY 1982, FY 1983 and FY 1984; and $35 million for FY 1985. However, actual appropriations have continued the downward trend that Title II-B has experienced since the late 1960s. From a high of $8.3 million in 1969, appropriations for Title II-B have fallen to the 1983 low of $880,000—with the most significant decreases coming at a time when the scope of the program was actually being expanded. Since the amount specifically dedicated to research and development under Title II-B is only one third of the total appropriation, the federal funding actually available for research into "more economical and efficient information delivery, cooperative efforts (such as networking), developmental projects, and improvement of information technology" has become practically negligible.

NATIONAL SCIENCE FOUNDATION

Established as an independent federal agency by Congress in 1950, the National Science Foundation (NSF) is charged with promoting the progress of science through the support of research and education. Through its various divisions and discretionary grant programs, NSF attempts to:

• Increase the nation's base of scientific knowledge and strengthen its ability to conduct scientific research;

• Encourage research in areas that can lead to improvements in economic growth, energy supply and use, productivity, and environmental quality;

• Promote international cooperation through science; and

• Develop and help implement science education programs that can better prepare the nation for meeting the challenges of the decades ahead.

Division of Information Science and Technology

From 1958 to 1978, NSF supported information and library-related projects through its Office of Science Information Service (OSIS). In 1978 responsibility for the dissemination of scientific information was removed from OSIS and returned to NSF's individual research divisions, and a new division was created to support projects in the rapidly growing field of information science. This new division, the Division of Information Science and Technology (DIST), was located in the Directorate for Scientific, Technological and International Affairs. In 1981 NSF was reorganized again, and DIST was relocated to the Directorate for Biological, Behavioral and Social Sciences.

Since the 1981 reorganization, DIST has supported basic and applied research in information science and technology through three related programs: Information Science, Information Technology and Information Impact. (These three program areas replaced the five more specific categories that had been used previously: Standards and Measures, Structure of Information, Behavioral Aspects of Information Transfer, Infometrics and Information Technology.) As of early 1983, it is still too early to tell how the reassignment of DIST and the reorganization of the program will affect its activities.

Goals and Objectives

According to a recent NSF program announcement, the goals of DIST are to:

• Increase understanding of the properties and structure of information and information transfer;

• Contribute to the store of scientific and technical knowledge which can be applied in the design of information systems; and

• Improve understanding of the economic and other impacts of information science and technology.

The program announcement also outlines the goals and responsibilities of the three program areas within DIST. According to NSF, the Information Science Program "is concerned with increasing the fundamental knowledge necessary for understanding information processes." NSF defines information science as the study of "the structure of information and its transfer." Research topics in this area include the study of information collections and collection organization, the relationship between information and knowledge, statistical theories of information, and patterns of information perception.

The Information Technology Program "is concerned with research on the application of information science to the design of advanced information systems." Information technology is broadly defined as computer and communications technologies and their applications, and research in this program area generally concentrates on the development and uses of information systems.

The Information Impact Program is charged with gaining "a scientific understanding of the economic aspects of the production, distribution, and use of information, and of the increasingly pervasive aspects of the diverse applications of advanced information technology." In other words, the Information Impact Program is concerned with the effects of information technologies on all areas of society. Research in this area includes studies of ways that information technology affects productivity and investigations of various procedures for modeling information flow.

Proposal Process

Proposals for the discretionary grants administered by DIST may be submitted by academic institutions, by profit-making and nonprofit organizations, or by consortia groups. Generally, proposals may be submitted at any time, and they are reviewed by both NSF staff and outside reviewers. The review process usually takes six to eight months.

Funding Levels

Since the divisional reorganization of 1981, total funding for the three DIST programs has held between $5 million and $6 million. As Table 5.2 indicates, appropriations dipped in FY 1982, but rose slightly in FY 1983. If NSF's budget request for FY 1984 is approved, total DIST appropriations will increase to $6.1 million.

Activities and Impact

Although the various NSF divisions fund a wide range of research projects, most have little or no immediate impact on libraries. DIST has, however, supported several studies,

Table 5.2 Federal Allocations to the Division of Information Science and Technology, National Science Foundation, Fiscal Years 1981 to 1983 (in thousands)

Program	Appropriation			
	1981	1982	1983	Total
Information Science	$4,272	$4,000	$4,000	$12,272
Information Technology	286	400	597	1,283
Information Impact	1,386	800	800	2,986
TOTAL	$5,944	$5,200	$5,397	$16,541

Source: Division of Information Science and Technology, National Science Foundation, 1983.

centers and projects that are of direct interest to library professionals. Some examples include:

• The 1975 Fry/White study titled "Economics and Interaction of the Publisher-Library Relationship in the Production and Use of Scholarly and Research Journals";

• The Northeast Academic Science Information Center in New England;

• The Investigations of Computer-aided Document Search Strategies conducted at the Massachusetts Institute of Technology; and

• A study of the Economics of Information Transfer Using Resource Sharing Networks-Network Modeling Simulation.

In many of these cases, DIST has supported library research and development for which no other public funding was available. In the future, DIST's role in library development will depend on NSF's federal appropriation levels, and on the manner in which NSF interprets its policy and program goals.

NATIONAL LIBRARY OF MEDICINE, EXTRAMURAL GRANTS PROGRAM

The National Library of Medicine (NLM) is heavily involved in research and development projects necessary to support its own activities. These internal programs are housed at the Lister Hill National Center for Biomedical Communications, and they are described in Chapter 3.

In addition to its internal research activities, NLM also administers an Extramural Grants Program that is funded through the Medical Library Assistance Act (MLAA). The general support available to medical libraries through NLM and the Extramural Grants Program was described in Chapter 4.

In 1979 three new discretionary grant programs related to research in biomedical communications were initiated. These are: New Investigator Awards, which provide funds to researchers who are seeking support for personally designed research projects for the first time; Research Career Development Awards, which support researchers who are more established and who have demonstrated outstanding potential for making contributions to health-related information science; and the Computers-in-Medicine Program, which supports studies of computer applications in health-sciences communication.

In 1980 Congress appropriated $1.3 million in special funding for the Computers-in-Medicine Program. This permitted the funding of 10 new research projects in the areas of knowledge representation, data base management and clinical decision making.

NATIONAL ENDOWMENT FOR THE HUMANITIES

Another funding agency that has played an important role in library development is the National Endowment for the Humanities (NEH). Created in 1965, NEH is an independent grant-making agency that supports projects of research, education and public activity in the humanities. According to the Endowment's governing legislation, the term ''humanities'' includes, but is not limited to, the study of the following: languge, both modern and classical; linguistics; literature; history; jurisprudence; philosophy; archaeology; the history, criticism, theory and practice of the arts; those aspects of the social sciences that have humanistic content and employ humanistic methods; and the study and application of the humanities to the environment.

Grants are made to individuals, groups or institutions such as schools, colleges, universities, museums, public television stations and libraries. All grants are discretionary in nature. An application must be made to NEH, and individual applicants compete for available funds. In addition, most NEH divisions provide pre-application counseling. Although support for humanities-related library activities is available from all five of NEH's divisions and its Office of Challenge Grants (see below), most of the NEH funding for library development has come from the Division of General Programs and the Division of Research Programs.

Division of General Programs

The Office of Program Development in the Division of General Programs includes a section devoted to libraries, the Libraries Humanities Project (LHP). This project awards grants to strengthen programs that stimulate and respond to public interest in the humanities, to enhance the ability of library staff to plan and implement these programs, and to increase the public's awareness and use of a library's existing humanities resources. Funded programs are not research in the strict sense, since they normally function as demonstration projects.

Examples of projects funded by LHP include:

• Oklahoma Department of Libraries, Oklahoma City, OK: $400,000 to improve library services and promote quality humanities programs stressing Oklahoma's multicultural heritage;

• Chicago Public Library, Chicago: $100,300 to support a year-long program designed to give out-of-school adults the opportunity to learn more about the literature of the many foreign cultures represented in the ethnic populations of Chicago;

• Southwestern Library Association, Denton, TX: $177,982 to present public programming in oral history in southwestern communities; and

• Pikes Peak Regional Library District, Colorado Springs, CO: $89,382 to support a series of lectures by 13 authors who have published works on the historical, literary and social development of the Pikes Peak region. The library provided exhibit material, bibliographies, walking tours and lectures with panel discussions.

Division of Research Programs

The Division of Research Programs provides support for research projects in the humanities, for the preparation of important research tools and for the editing of significant humanistic texts. Within the Division of Research Programs, the Research Resources Program is designed to make raw research materials more accessible to scholars. Its goals are to increase access to materials through projects that address national problems in the archival and library field, through projects that serve as models in systems development and library automation, and through processing grants that are used to catalog, inventory or otherwise gain bibliographic control of significant research collections. The Division of Research Programs also administers the Preservation and Conservation Project, a program that supports demonstration projects designed to preserve important materials or to test new preservation technologies, and the United States Newspaper Projects, a coordinated effort to catalog and preserve newspaper files that are in danger of disintegration.

Specific activities that have received support through the Division of Research Programs include:

• New York Public Library, New York: $4.8 million to support the National Services of Research Libraries, a program for document and pamphlet preservation, and NYPL's other nationally available humanities services;

• St. John's University, Collegeville, MN: $200,000 to fund the microfilming of ancient manuscripts of the Ethiopian Orthodox Church by the Hill Monastic Manuscript Library;

• Ohio College Library Center, Columbus, OH: $60,000 to develop a non-Roman alphabet capability for online library services;

• Newberry Library, Chicago: a $900,000 grant for library operations; and

• Council on Library Resources, Washington, DC: $200,000 to fund a computerized bibliographic network for libraries.

Most notable among recent research grants has been NEH's support for the Bibliographic Service Development Program (BSDP). In 1981, NEH joined with the Council on Library Resources and other foundations to provide $5 million in developmental funding. In 1983 funding for BSDP was extended through 1986. The goals of the program are to promote: 1) widespread availability of bibliographic services; 2) improvement of bibliographic products; and 3) control of the cost of bibliographic processes for libraries.

Office of Planning and Policy Assessment

Additional projects may be funded through the Office of Planning and Policy Assessment, the NEH office charged with determining national needs in the humanities and developing new or improved programs to meet those needs. The office supports projects in data collection and analysis, program evaluation and policy analysis.

Office of Challenge Grants

The Challenge Grant Program was initiated in 1977 "to stimulate increased support for humanities institutions from private citizens, business and labor organizations, state and local governments, and civic and other groups by offering one federal dollar for every three raised in the private sector." In 1982 the Division of Research Programs launched a special challenge-grant program for independent research libraries. It awarded 13 matching grants ranging from $100,000 to $2 million for a total of $5.3 million. NEH instituted the program because: "1) independent research libraries collect, preserve and promote research in important records of the past; 2) these libraries have demonstrated that they can carry out their mission intelligently and efficiently; and 3) they need substantial financial assistance to continue providing their basic services." Recipients of the special challenge grants include the Library Company of Philadelphia, the American Philosophical Society and the New York Public Library.

Other NEH Programs

Other divisions within NEH provide funding that is sometimes made available to libraries. For example, the Education Division may award grants to libraries directly or to libraries as part of a larger university effort to develop new curricula or educational materials. Or NEH grants may be made available to support humanities institutes in which library resources play a role. Some recipients of this type of grant include the Folger Shakespeare Library (Washington, DC) and the Newberry Library (Chicago).

In addition, support for libraries is sometimes made available through the Fellowship Division, the Division of State Programs and the Special Projects Program. The Fellowship Division awards grants to scholars, teachers and members of nonacademic professions to pursue studies in humanities-related areas. Institutions such as the Huntington Library (San Moreno, CA) and the American Antiquarian Society have housed NEH fellows. The Division of State Programs provides funding to citizens' committees in each state to carry on the mission of NEH at the local level. Finally, the Special Projects Program, a section of the Division of General Programs, supports innovative projects that are not covered by any other NEH division. Library participation in projects funded by these last two programs depends to a large extent on the imaginations of individual libraries and their successful cooperation with local groups.

Role of NEH in Library Development

Few of the NEH programs support basic or applied research. They do, however, provide a means for libraries to develop demonstration projects, extend their research capability and establish new sources of revenue.

As with the National Science Foundation, the future role of NEH in library development will depend on its continuing ability to fund important projects. Its mission is to provide the dollars needed for research and development, and to a lesser extent for operations. In the past, NEH has proved to be a valuable resource and has supported some critical library-related projects. It has also shown itself willing to join with other funding agencies to provide cooperative support for large undertakings.

DEPARTMENT OF EDUCATION, NATIONAL INSTITUTE OF EDUCATION

The National Institute of Education (NIE) was created by Congress in 1972 as the primary federal agency for educational research and development. Its mission is to promote educational equity and to improve the quality of educational practice. To achieve these goals, NIE supports a variety of research and dissemination activities.

NIE is housed in the U.S. Department of Education and reports to the Assistant Secretary for Educational Research and Improvement. Its activities are organized into three broad program areas: Teaching and Learning, Educational Policy and Organization and Dissemination and Improvement of Practice.

Although NIE funds research specifically directed to the educational community, some small amounts of support have been provided to library-related projects. For example, NIE has supported R&D activities to improve the scope and quality of information services available to educators and to develop and distribute research publications geared to the needs of practicing educators. NIE has also provided support to improve the Educational Resources Information Center (ERIC), one of the federal information services described in Chapter 3.

Even though ERIC itself is an important information service, and even though other NIE projects do relate to library and information services, NIE cannot be seen as a major funder of general library and information-related research. Nevertheless, it is included here to provide as complete a picture as possible of potential federal research resources.

NATIONAL COMMISSION ON LIBRARIES AND INFORMATION SCIENCE

Although the National Commission on Libraries and Information Science (NCLIS) is sometimes seen as a funding agency for research projects, budget limitations and conflicting priorities have kept its role in this area quite small. Indeed, NCLIS sees itself more as a planning and policy-making agency than it does as a supporter of research. An examination of publications issued by NCLIS since its establishment in 1970 reveals that many are products of task forces, while others have clear political implications.

The legislation establishing the Commission was quite specific about its primary role: "The Commission shall have the primary responsibility for developing or recommending overall plans for, and advising the appropriate governments and agencies on, the provision of library and information services adequate to meet the needs of the people of the United States." To achieve this goal, NCLIS is authorized to conduct a number of activities, only one of which is to "promote research and development." For FY 1983, the Commission's federal appropriation was $674,000.

The fact that promoting research and development activities is subsidiary to the central responsibility of recommending action suggests that research is not the central mission of NCLIS. Research is commissioned when it is necessary for NCLIS to arrive at informed recommendations, but there is no funding set aside for research as such. When research contracts are available, they are awarded to individual contractors on a sole-source basis, or to organizations or individuals through the request-for-proposals process.

The planning and policy-making activities of NCLIS are discussed more fully in Chapter 6.

CONCLUSION

As the 1980s unfold, there appears to be a federal commitment to providing even more funds for defense-related research and development, and a concurrent commitment to reducing support for research in other areas. Sponsors of this move appear to feel that benefits from defense-related R&D will "trickle down" to the public at large.

In the 1940s, it took a war to convince the nation that scientific and technological development merited the attention of the federal government. Today, there is an equally significant change occurring, as the world economy moves from an industrial to an information base. With this shift, support for information research has become a necessary component in the federal government's program to "promote the common defense" and "provide for the general welfare." In the current era, our national defense rests as surely on information systems and communications capabilities as it does on the size of a deliverable warhead.

Moreover, the nation's industrial and economic life has become inextricably linked to information technology and services. Information technology provides ways to improve industry productivity, while at the same time generating new product markets. But competition from Japan and West Germany is already stiff, and it can be expected to get even stiffer. If U.S. industries are to compete effectively with their foreign counterparts, a much greater national investment in information-related research is imperative. In addition, more effective diffusion of this information must be achieved.

Libraries, in their various forms, are largely responsible for the diffusion of knowledge. True, they occupy only a small corner of the information world. Nevertheless, libraries provide services that are essential if the nation is to retain its leading role in the new information economy. To the degree that libraries can be made to function more effectively, they will contribute to national growth and development.

The situation is somewhat ironic. The very research that is so vital to developing information industries will also enable libraries to perform their functions better. At the same time, one of the library's primary functions is to make information and research more widely available.

The efforts by federal agencies described in this chapter have achieved much, but they have not done enough. At present, following the program cutbacks of the early 1980s, federal support for information-related research is dangerously low. We can only hope for a reversal of this trend, and for federal recognition of the critical role that libraries and information services will play in shaping the nation's future.

FOOTNOTES

1. Harold Vagtborg, *Research and American Industrial Development* (New York: Pergamon Press, 1976).

2. U.S. Department of Commerce, Bureau of the Census, *Statistical Abstract of the United States, 1981* (Washington, DC: Government Printing Office, 1981).

3. *Ibid.*

4. Cuadra Associates, Inc., *A Library and Information Science Research Agenda for the 1980s.* Final report of a project conducted for the U.S. Department of Education, Office of Libraries and Learning Technologies (Santa Monica, CA: Cuadra Associates, Inc., 1982).

5. U.S. Department of Commerce, Bureau of Industrial Economics, *1982 U.S. Industrial Outlook for 200 Industries with Projections for 1986* (Washington, DC: Government Printing Office, 1982).

6. Cuadra Associates, Inc., op. cit.

7. Miriam A. Drake, "The Economics of Library Networks" in *Networks for Networkers,* ed. by Barbara Evans Markuson and Blanche Woolls (New York: Neal-Schuman Publishers, 1980).

8. National Science Foundation, National Science Board, *Science Indicators* (Washington, DC: Government Printing Office, 1978).

9. Helena M. Strauch, "Entrepreneurship in the Information Industry" in *Careers in Information,* ed. by Jane F. Spivack. (White Plains, NY: Knowledge Industry Publications, Inc., 1982).

6

Planning and Policy Making

Presumably, planning is an essential part of all government decision making, and policy is a natural result of decisions made and actions taken. Nevertheless, issues flowing from planning and policy making have come to be regarded separately in recent years, as attention has focused on the growing body of policy known as "information policy."

In the United States, "information policy" is actually a set of interrelated laws and policies concerned with the creation, production, collection, management, distribution and retrieval of information. Their significance lies in the fact that they profoundly affect the manner in which an individual in a society, indeed a society itself, makes political, economic and social choices.

A complete analysis of information policy issues, options and consequences must consider two related trends: a convergence in information technology and a divergence in the uses and applications of information itself. That is, as computer and communications technologies have become increasingly indistinguishable, information policy decisions have begun to have direct implications for all aspects of government and society: the environment, energy, transportation, employment, economic development, health, education and international relations. As a result, many informed observers, both within and outside government, feel that the primary political issues of the 1980s are, in fact, information policy issues.

This chapter provides an introduction to federal information policy. In the long run, this policy, or set of policies, may well have a greater impact on the basic mission of libraries than any other single activity of the federal government. Thus, the chapter explores the development of federal information policy as a special area of concern, tracing the primary issues involved, describing relevant legislation, and examining the roles of the agencies that enforce the laws and regulations.

Within the context of prevailing information policy, this chapter also looks briefly at library planning and policy making that takes place within the federal government. Specifically, it examines the planning activities of the Department of Education and the National Commission on Libraries and Information Science (NCLIS), comparing their different approaches and evaluating their impact and effectiveness.

Although library policy and information policy are separated for purposes of discussion, they have become increasingly interdependent. This chapter concludes with a discussion of the interrelationships that exist today and that are likely to arise in the future.

INTRODUCTION TO INFORMATION POLICY

The United States was founded on the belief that a democratic society requires an educated and informed electorate. Indeed, the belief in diversity of opinion and the free market of ideas is embedded in the First Amendment to the Constitution.

In addition to enunciating these basic beliefs, the Constitution provided for government involvement in the communication process by granting Congress the power "to establish Post Offices and Post Roads." Although this early communications network grew slowly, it provided the nation's primary means of communication until the introduction of the telegraph (1837) and the telephone (1876). The electronic age heralded by these inventions was accompanied by increased involvement of the federal government in the establishment of what may now be seen as early information policy.

Defining Information Policy

The term "information policy" was not used until the early 1970s. At that time, a number of organizations and individuals began to build on the work of Fritz Machlup, the author of a landmark 1962 study that identified a large and growing knowledge-based industry in the United States. Since Machlup's study, Daniel Bell has described the birth of the "post-industrial society"; Marc Porat has concluded, after exhaustive research, that over 50% of the gross national product of the United States is derived from information-related activities; Alvin Toffler has warned us that we may soon be swept away by "the third wave"; and John Nesbitt has described how the growing importance of information is the driving force behind what he calls "megatrends."

Identifying Policy Issues

In recent years, several notable attempts have been made to classify the primary issues to be considered in this large and somewhat amorphous area. In 1976 *National Information Policy,* a report to the president by the Domestic Council on the Right of Privacy, identified five issue clusters covering 15 individual information-policy issues. Several years later, in an unpublished report, the National Telecommunications and Information Agency (NTIA) identified seven issue areas. In 1979 the Information Industry Association listed some 75 issues in nine key areas.

In 1980 and 1981, NTIA issued two special reports: *The Foundations of United States Information Policy* and *Issues in Information Policy.* Significantly, the two NTIA reports group information policy issues into questions concerning "individual liberties and societal welfare" and questions regarding "economic efficiency and equity." A third set of policy issues, alluded to but not discussed, is concerned with international information questions.

A review of the 1976 report reveals that the five groupings used by the Domestic Council on the Right of Privacy, while more exploratory and functional in nature, are similar to the NTIA categories. They are: government information collection, transfer and dissemination; information in commerce: a resource for public good and private gain; the interaction between technology and government; international implications of information policies and developments; and preparing for the information age.

Political Issues

Although there is nothing magic about any one classification scheme, most of those that have been identified may by viewed from the perspective of two of the overarching political issues described in Chapter 2: individual rights and property rights. Posed as conflicts between competing values, they have been described as: 1) the freedom of the individual versus the good of the society as a whole and 2) private sector interests versus public sector responsibilities.

The following sections describe the specific information policy issues found in both these areas. As indicated in the more general consideration of political theory and social values covered in Chapter 2, there is a high degree of ambiguity and tension within each area. Moreover, as competing factions and interests jockey for position, balance between the issues becomes increasingly difficult to achieve.

INDIVIDUAL RIGHTS

Ideally, the federal government functions as both a defender of individual freedoms and a protector of the general welfare. To safeguard individual freedom, the First Amendment provides specific protections for free expression of ideas and opinions by individuals in our open, democratic society. By implication, the First Amendment also suggests that the government has a responsibility to distribute political information and information about its activities, so citizens have the knowledge they need to make informed decisions. These basic principles have been reenforced by statute, regulation and case law.

Collection and Disclosure of Information

In spite of constitutional support for the principle of free access to information, there are some important restrictions that limit the application of the public's First Amendment "right to know." Specifically, open access is generally applied to government information sources and not to individuals or private organizations. While there are some exceptions to this rule, including regulations that require organizations to disclose information about activities that could adversely affect the general public, disclosure requirements for private groups remain quite limited.

In addition, the government itself is excused from providing certain types of information that might in some way endanger the general public, or some portion of the general public. Information related to national security, obscene material and some types of commercial data are examples of information that the government is not required to distribute.

Finally, the government itself has a right to collect certain privately held information when the general welfare requires it. For example, as part of their operations, the Internal Revenue Service and the Census Bureau collect data that is sometimes of a sensitive nature. Nevertheless, even here, government access is limited by law and the use of information beyond the purpose for which it was originally collected is restricted. These protective policies have been developed to safeguard civil liberties and individual and corporate property rights.

Conflicts, Rights and Responsibilities

Between the extremes of individual freedom and the need to protect the general welfare, there is a vast sea of misunderstanding, conflict, tension and ambiguity. Balance is difficult to achieve, and unresolved issues proliferate. Moreover, the entire bundle of issues is growing in size, scope and significance as technological advances render information of all types easier to store and access.

The conflict between openness and restriction of government information is not easy to resolve. The government has rights and responsibilities, but so do individuals and private organizations. For the purposes of this discussion, the issues involved in this fundamental conflict are presented as aspects of two perspectives: the responsibility of the federal government to distribute and provide access to information of a public nature, and the limits imposed on the government for the protection of individual privacy.

DISTRIBUTION AND ACCESS

As described in Chapter 3, the government has historically pursued a policy of actively distributing information about federal programs and activities. Reports on federal activities are published by the Government Printing Office, and they are distributed through the National Technical Information Service and the Depository Library System. In addition, numerous agencies maintain public information offices, members of Congress distribute information to their constituents, and federal subsidies for public libraries encourage the use of federally produced information.

The federal "open information" policy is reflected in several statutes that require federal agencies to disclose information upon request. Two relatively recent acts, the Freedom of Information Act (FOIA) and the Government in the Sunshine Act (Sunshine Act) are probably the most significant.

Freedom of Information Act

The Freedom of Information Act was originally passed in 1966. Its purpose is to promote public access to government–held information by requiring that each federal agency publish and actively distribute some materials, make other materials available for inspection, and respond to public questions and requests. Information that must be actively distributed includes: 1) descriptions of the agency's office organization and procedures for interaction with the public; 2) explanations of all formal and informal functions and procedures; and 3) statements of general policy and substantive rules. Information that must be made available for public inspection and copying includes final adjudicative opinions, interpretations of policy, and staff manuals and instructions that affect the public.

All other information must be disclosed upon request, unless it falls within one of the nine areas that have disclosure exemptions. The exempted areas are: 1) information that is authorized to be kept secret in the interests of national defense or foreign policy; 2) internal agency personnel rules and practices; 3) information specifically exempted from disclosure by statute; 4) certain trade secrets and commercial information; 5) inter- and intra-agency communications that reflect an agency's deliberative process; 6) certain personal information; 7) certain investigatory records compiled for law enforcement purposes; 8) financial regulatory reports; and 9) certain geological and geophysical information.

Government in the Sunshine Act

The Sunshine Act was passed in 1976. Its purpose is to make federal information more readily available by requiring that certain federal meetings be open to the public. Although the Sunshine Act requires that "every portion of every meeting of an agency shall be open to public observation," agencies covered by the Act can close a meeting if it is "likely" to disclose information included in one of 10 disclosure exemptions. These exemptions are similar to those listed for the FOIA.

RESTRAINTS ON PUBLIC ACCESS TO INFORMATION

The federal government is not required to provide individuals with access to all types of information. Moreover, the federal courts have judged that some categories of information are not protected by the First Amendment. Over the years, this conflict between individual rights and social welfare has proven particularly difficult to resolve.

As the exemptions listed for the Freedom of Information Act indicate, the federal government is generally free to restrict the public's "right to know" when it determines that the disclosure or distribution of certain information would threaten the general welfare. In recent years, however, considerable controversy has centered around the criteria used to determine whether information falls into this category. After several Supreme Court decisions and extensive legislative debate, the following five objectives are now considered valid reasons for restricting public access to information under most circumstances: "1) national security, 2) protection of the public from deceptive or misleading commercial information, 3) protection of personal information, 4) protection of copyright, and 5) protection of the public from offensive or obscene information."[1] Protection of information about individuals is considered in the section of this chapter that deals with privacy issues, and copyright protection is examined in the section dealing with information policy and property rights. The other areas are discussed below.

National Security

Federal information is often classified in the name of national security. While few would argue with the notion that national security ought to be protected, it is unclear to many how a determination is made concerning which disclosures might constitute a security risk. Even the statutes, regulations and legal opinions that govern this important area are ambiguous. For example, Executive Order 12065 (1978) governs the classification of official documents and makes information confidential if disclosure "could reasonably be expected to cause damage to the national security." But the Order fails to provide any criteria by which agencies and the courts may determine "damage." Moreover, the president has a constitutional obligation to withhold information if, in his opinion, its disclosure would compromise national security.[2]

In the wake of Watergate, Viet Nam and assorted controversial actions taken by the Environmental Protection Agency, the public has become increasingly suspicious of government secrecy in the name of national security. It is often difficult to know what information would truly endanger the nation were it to become public, and what information has been classified for purely political reasons. The balance is difficult to strike.

Commercial Information

While national security considerations are usually concerned with access to and distribution of government–held information, federal information policy also establishes the right of the government to impede the flow of information among individuals, and thereby limit individual First Amendment rights, if such intervention is in the public interest.

To many, the regulation of deceptive commercial information seems non-controversial. Indeed, it would appear that some sort of federal regulation is the only way to ensure integrity in the marketplace. For many years, the federal government, through the Federal Trade Commission, has been authorized to intervene when advertising is misleading. Some corporate representatives maintain, however, that such intervention is unnecessary. They claim that regulations are burdensome, that dissatisfied consumers have recourse through the courts, and that the marketplace will sort itself out (with erroneous information exposed by the deceitful company's competitors). Since 1980 the prevailing philosophy in Washington has been that less regulation is better, and the regulatory powers of the Federal Trade Commission in this important area have been curtailed.

Obscenity

There is probably no area in which government information policy strives to "protect the public" that is more controversial than the area of obscenity. A number of problems make restriction of "obscene" material markedly different from restrictions imposed on other types of information.

To most Americans, any dilution of First Amendment guarantees is perceived as a potential threat to our democratic form of government. Nevertheless, the public usually accepts restrictions when they are regarded as necessary for the general welfare. This is obviously the case in each area described above. In the case of obscene material, however, "harm" becomes a matter of personal interpretation based on individually held, and often conflicting, moral values.

To compound the problem, the legal definition of obscenity is ambiguous and relies on individual judgment. According to the 1957 Supreme Court decision in the landmark case of Roth v. United States, obscenity is defined as: "Whether to the average person, applying contemporary community standards, the dominant theme of the material taken as a whole appeals to prurient interest." In subsequent decisions, the Supreme Court has gone on to specify certain categories of material that could be considered obscene, but it has remained committed to the "community standards" guideline issued in the Roth case.

Many feel that local authorities should not have the power to decide what is and is not obscene. Certainly, this is the only instance in which a decision of such magnitude, hinging as it does on an interpretation of the First Amendment, is made in such a parochial manner with so little federal guidance. Moreover, at a time when mass communications systems carry entertainment and information programming to the entire country, it seems unrealistic and somewhat reactionary to place decisions concerning freedom of speech that affect all citizens in the hands of local community groups and factions.

CURRENT TRENDS IN FEDERAL INFORMATION DISTRIBUTION AND ACCESS

Since 1981 steps have been taken by the Reagan administration to curtail the ability and responsibility of the federal government to provide information to the public. While many of these recent actions have been in the form of administrative decisions and regulations, they have the effect of law and together constitute a major shift in U.S. information policy in the important area of distribution and access.

The Reagan administration has justified its policies on the grounds of cost reduction or the elimination of unnecessary regulation, or as steps necessary to protect national security. Whether one believes these justifications or not, there is no doubt that the administration's actions have resulted in a deliberate shift of power from the public to the private sector. This in turn has resulted in the erosion of the public's ability to retrieve the information necessary to make informed decisions, in what amounts to an outright attack on the principle that access to information about government is critical for public participation in the political process.

ALA Chronology

Alarmed by this trend, the American Library Association has produced a partial chronology of recent actions related to the distribution of government information. ALA issued its initial listing in January, 1982. An updated version was released in July of 1982, and additional reports have been published as events have occurred. Because actions limiting access to government information are cumulative, and because events taken singly may appear relatively insignificant, the entire chronology prepared by the ALA Washington Office is presented in Appendix A.

The events summarized in Appendix A can be grouped into several categories, according to whether the initiatives result in: the reduction of information by or about the federal government through the publication of fewer items; the reduction of the capacity of the government to provide information; the reclassification of numerous reports and documents; the reinterpretation of the Freedom of Information Act, thereby downgrading the federal responsibility to provide information; or the shift of federal information distribution rights and responsibilities to the private sector. (This last effort will be addressed in more detail later in this chapter in the section on property rights.)

Paperwork Reduction Act of 1980

Many of the Reagan administration's actions have been initiated under the authority of the Paperwork Reduction Act of 1980. This legislation, which was signed into law by President Carter, was originally intended to ensure that the federal government use information technologies in a manner that "improves service delivery and program management, increases productivity, reduces waste and fraud, and, whenever practicable and appropriate, reduces the information processing burden for the federal government and for persons who provide information to the federal government."

Although few have taken exception to these goals, some analysts have objected to the manner in which the Act has been administered. The Paperwork Reduction Act gave the Office of Management and Budget (OMB) "unprecedented authority to control the flow of federal information."[3] It established an Office of Information and Regulatory Affairs to be administered by a director empowered to:

> . . . develop and implement federal information policies, principles, standards
> and guidelines and provide direction and oversee the review and approval of
> information collection requests, the reduction of the paper work burden,
> federal statistical activities, records management activities, privacy of records,
> interagency sharing of information, and acquisition and use of automatic
> data processing telecommunications, and other technology for managing in-
> formation resources.

The law further specifies that "There shall be no judicial review of any kind of the director's decision to approve or not to act upon a collection of information requirement contained in an agency rule." This last provision, in effect, places the director above the law, a circumstance that troubled many even before the bill was passed.[4]

PRIVACY RIGHTS

Balanced against the belief that information by or about the government should be widely disseminated is the conviction that individuals, and in some instances corporate interests, have a right to privacy. Since most of the policy issues concerning information generated by corporations turn on a consideration of property rights, the relationship between the government and the private sector in this important area is also relevant here.

The legal foundation for individual privacy rights is found in common law and in the Fourth and Fifth Amendments. The Fourth Amendment protects individuals against unreasonable searches and seizures and the Fifth Amendment guarantees due process. Until the 1960s, these protections were deemed adequate because, for the most part, individuals rather than computers maintained control of records of a sensitive nature.

Technology and Privacy

Today, large record-keeping organizations both within and outside the government use sophisticated computer systems to maintain large banks of personal information. Because individuals cannot get a job or loan, enter a hospital or college, or own a home or car without relinquishing some personal information, the data banks continue to grow and individuals involved have little control over how the information is subsequently used.

In addition to the standard record-keeping activities performed by finance companies, credit bureaus, insurance companies, credit card companies, the Internal Revenue Service, the CIA, the FBI, government welfare agencies and the Census Bureau, there is another, more Orwellian development that threatens to erode individual privacy even further. In recent years, surveillance devices have become much more sophisticated. Lie detectors and other "truth monitors" have developed to the point where they can be used without the subject's knowledge; and home-based online information services, such as videotext, electronic funds transfer and electronic mail, provide private corporations with a wide range of information about individual users.

Growing Public Concern

A survey conducted by Louis Harris and Associates, Inc. in December 1978 revealed that 64% of the American people were concerned about threats to their personal privacy, a figure up significantly from the 47% reported one year earlier. Although more recent information is not available, the percentage of people concerned about personal privacy has undoubtedly increased in recent years.

Even in 1978, however, one out of three of the people surveyed believed that our society is already close to conditions described in Orwell's *Nineteen Eighty-Four,* in which "virtually all personal privacy had been lost and the government knew almost everything that everyone was doing."[5]

Privacy Act of 1974

Although there are several statutes that contain provisions protecting individual privacy rights in specific areas (e.g., Fair Credit Reporting Act, Family Educational Rights and Privacy Act of 1974), the primary piece of legislation concerned with privacy protection is the Privacy Act of 1974. The Privacy Act prohibits federal agencies from revealing information of a personal nature unless the disclosure has been approved by the individual or falls within one of the eleven exceptions. In addition, the Act:

> . . . permits agencies to disclose information only if it is accurate, complete, timely, and relevant; it permits record subjects to see, copy and correct most information in their files; it places certain limits on federal collection of personal information; it requires federal agencies to meet certain information

management standards; and it requires federal agencies to publish descriptions of records systems containing personal information.[6]

Reactions to the Privacy Act have been mixed. Since it was the first statute to specify fair information practices to protect individual privacy, public reaction to the Act has special significance. Some analysts have pointed out that, together with the Freedom of Information Act, the Privacy Act has provided a balanced approach to the continuing problem of privacy versus freedom of information. Collectively, the laws make it clear that government-held information should be made public, as long as revealing the information would not violate an individual's right to privacy. In fact, one of the disclosure exemptions of the FOIA covers information "the disclosure of which would constitute a clearly unwarranted invasion of privacy."

Nevertheless, the Privacy Act has been criticized for its vagueness, its broad disclosure exemptions and its failure to establish adequate restraints on federal handling of personal information.[7] Moreover, it does not cover personal information files maintained in the private sector.

Privacy Protection Study Commission

In 1977 the Privacy Protection Study Commission sought to address the omissions and inadequacies of the Privacy Act. The *Report of the Study Commission* pointed out problems arising from the omnibus approach to information legislation contained in the Act, and recommended separate reform and regulation for different types of information-holding relationships. It articulated five characteristics of personal information that require attention from a policy perspective:

• There must be no personal data record-keeping systems whose existence is secret;

• There must be a way for an individual to find out what information about him is in a record and how it is used;

• There must be a way for an individual to prevent personal information obtained for one purpose from being used or made available for other purposes without his consent;

• There must be a way for an individual to correct or amend a record of indentifiable information about him; and

• Any organization creating, maintaining, using or disseminating records of identifiable personal data must assure its reliability for the intended use, and must take precautions to prevent its misuse.[8]

The report concluded that "we are faced with a slow but steady erosion of privacy which, if left unreversed, will take us in another generation to a position where the extent of our human rights and the vitality of our democracy will be jeopardized."[9]

Governing Principles

At present, information policy concerning privacy is based on two principles:

> Fair Information Practices. Standards must be provided for handling sensitive personal records. Individuals should be told what kind of information is being collected about them, how it will be used, and to whom it will be disclosed. They should be able to see and obtain a copy of the records and correct any errors. They should be told the basis for an adverse decision that may be based on recorded personal information. And they should be able to prevent improper disclosure of records pertaining to them.

> Limits on Government. Government access to and use of personal information must be limited and supervised so that power over information cannot be used to threaten individual liberties.[10]

The resolution of most privacy issues rests on a balanced consideration of individual rights and societal welfare. Both business and government have legitimate reasons for collecting and using information about individuals. Few, for instance, would suggest that a bank should be required to decide on loans without obtaining information regarding the credit worthiness of an individual. And few would argue that the Internal Revenue Service should be prevented from gathering information about an individual's income and expenditures. Most of us would, however, object to the distribution of unverified, possibly erroneous information about a person, or to the use of a telephone tap to gather information about an individual's personal activities.

Privacy issues are escalating in number and importance. The balance that existed for two centuries has been shaken by technological change and the centralization of power that the technology permits. Better federal laws are needed to fully protect individual rights of privacy.

PROPERTY RIGHTS

A discussion of federal information policy must examine the relationship between government and the private sector (including large and small businesses and, in some instances, private individuals) from an economic perspective. The structure of the U.S. economic system has a firm philosophical base. For information-related activities, this base includes a belief in the importance of diversity of information, or a "marketplace of ideas"; the importance of a free market to ensure competition in providing diversity; and a policy of government intervention only when fundamental principles or individual freedoms are threatened—that is, when the free market fails to operate.

The Free Market of Ideas

Many information policies flow from the conviction that a diverse marketplace of ideas provides a more vigorous and dynamic environment, offering individuals a greater variety of choices and opportunities. The primary means by which the federal government seeks this diversity is the "free market" of unimpeded trade. When the free market fails to operate, however, the federal government maintains diversity through regulation of the content of the information disseminated, regulation of the industries that produce and transmit information, and regulations promoting public access to communications channels. In some instances, the government may also step in and provide information directly.

Regulation of Information Content

Regulation of information content is most apparent in federal regulations governing television, radio, cable television and other electronic communications systems. The allocation of the electromagnetic spectrum used in TV and radio broadcasting is one of the most obvious federal regulatory activities in this area. Because broadcast frequencies are a limited commodity, and because the electromagnetic spectrum is considered a public resource, TV and radio stations do not own the frequencies on which they broadcast. Instead, the federal government licenses stations to use frequencies for specific periods of time, under the condition that they meet certain technical and programming requirements deemed to be "in the public interest."

Fairness Doctrine

One of the programming requirements used to make licensing decisions is contained in the Fairness Doctrine. Through this policy, the Federal Communications Commission (FCC) requires broadcasters to dedicate a portion of their time to a discussion of controversial issues, including issues of local importance. An opportunity for the expression of opposing viewpoints is also required.

The Fairness Doctrine is not without controversy. Some see a conflict between its provisions and the First Amendment's restriction on government interference with the press. In fact, Supreme Court decisions in this area appear to be somewhat contradictory. For example, although the Supreme Court affirmed the constitutionality of the Fairness Doctrine for the broadcasting industry in a 1969 decision, a 1974 decision found that a similar policy for print media was not constitutional. Citing these apparent contradictions, FCC Chairman Mark Fowler, a Reagan appointee, has called for the complete repeal of the Fairness Doctrine. A repeal would require Congressional approval, however, and to date Congress has refused to go along.

Information as a Commodity

In recent years, information has come to be viewed as a business commodity. As a result, information policy has become increasingly concerned with the property and ownership issues raised in information creation, the structure of information markets and information management. Although property rights for information products (books, films, TV programs, etc.) are established in patent and copyright law, advances in copying technology have made enforcement difficult, and piracy is rampant. In addition, although the need to regulate market and pricing structures flows from the nature of information technology itself, the information industry is so volatile that unregulated industries and regulated monopolies appear to be competing in the same market.

Moreover, many feel that the government itself is competing unfairly with private information industries, while others believe that the government is abandoning its responsibility to provide access to government produced information. Another set of issues involves the government's management and disclosure of information. As mentioned earlier, many actions that restrict public access to information are taken in the name of efficiency in government. This requires examination.

INFORMATION CREATION

Throughout our nation's history, as part of its commitment to diversity of thought, the federal government has adopted policies supporting the creation of information. Basically, there are two ways in which the federal government supports intellectual effort in this area: establishment of private property rights through the award of patents and copyrights, and the provision of direct subsidies for the creation of information.

Some observers see a fundamental policy conflict in this important area. That conflict has to do with the choice between the two forms of government intervention: copyright enforcement or direct subsidy. According to one argument, government subsidy introduces the possibility of manipulation of the content, while a continuing commitment to copyright protection encourages private creation of information. But royalty payments to copyright holders limit distribution to those who can afford to pay, and information with a small audience is less likely to be produced no matter how important the material may be.[11]

While it is true that there is some conflict in goals embodied in these two approaches, it is not clear that they are mutually exclusive. On the contrary, given the fact that ours is a mixed economy, it would appear that some mix of strategies, as is currently the case, would protect the individual while looking after the best interests of society.

In spite of our current mixed approach however, the emphasis of the founding fathers was on the protection of individual property rights. According to Article I of the Constitution: "The Congress shall have power...to promote the progress of science and useful arts, by securing for limited times to authors and inventors the exclusive right to their respective writings and discoveries..." Working from this constitutional mandate, Congress passed the first copyright and patent acts in 1790, and the government has been trying to get it right through revisions and new copyright legislation ever since.

Basis for Copyright Protection

The basis for copyright protection is fairly straightforward. An individual has a right to enjoy the fruits of his labor, and the federal government has an interest in promoting the development of new information. But copyright is sometimes difficult to enforce, because information is different from other commodities. For example, information can be both sold and retained at the same time, the value of information is difficult to determine and information cannot be depleted.

Copyright and the New Technologies

New information technologies have compounded the problem, creating new definitions of "authorship." In addition, the technologies have raised new questions of ownership for products such as computer programs and computer-generated products. One particularly relevant incident occurred in 1982, when OCLC copyrighted the format of its data base. Challenges to this claim are almost assured, but as of early 1983 no action had taken place.

Other technology has provided the means of copying information products rapidly and cheaply. Although printed, recorded and broadcast materials have received most of the analysis to date, it is almost assured that the greatest controversy is likely to surround copying of computer programs and data bases. Computer programs are generally expensive to purchase, but quite cheap and inexpensive to copy. As a result, the temptation to copy is difficult to resist. Indeed, most software manufacturers readily acknowledge that piracy is one of their most pressing problems.

For data base providers, "downloading" (the online equivalent of piracy) has become an equally troublesome problem. It has become quite a simple thing for a data base user to download a file into his or her own computer. Once in the local computer, the data base may be searched repeatedly, with or without payment being made to the data base producer.

Fair Use

Several issues of particular interest to libraries relate to the interpretation of the "fair use" doctrine. Fair use refers to conditions under which a work or part of a work may be copied or used without the consent of the author. In the United States, this doctrine has been a part of case law since 1909, when Congress decided to leave interpretation to the courts. In the Copyright Revision Act of 1976, however, fair use was specifically defined as use "of a copyrighted work, including such use by reproduction...for purposes such as criticism, comment, news reporting, teaching (including multiple copies for classroom use), scholarship, or research." In addition, the Act established four criteria for determining fair use in individual cases:

1. The purpose and character of the use, including whether such use is of a commercial nature or is for nonprofit educational purposes;

2. The nature of the copyrighted work;

3. The amount and substantiality of the portion used in relation to the copyrighted work as a whole; and

4. The effect of the use upon the potential market for or value of the copyrighted work.

While these criteria are useful in making fair use determinations, they are not without ambiguity, and debates continue on several fronts. In particular, publishers and librarians argue about the impact of networking and other cooperative efforts on library purchasing of materials. On one hand, librarians claim that the determining limitation is their frozen or declining budgets, and that interlibrary loan and other sharing activities broaden the range of information made available to the library users. On the other hand, publishers claim that many libraries abuse fair use, substituting systematic photocopying for the purchase of periodicals or other publications.

This debate has recently erupted into outright warfare as several publishers have filed copyright suits against libraries. In a related action, off-air taping of television broadcasts became a volatile topic when a California court, in a suit by program producers against the Sony Corporation, held that off-air taping of TV programs in private homes is a violation of copyright. The decision was overturned on appeal, and the case will be heard before the Supreme Court sometime in 1983. Meanwhile, Congress is considering action of its own.

No matter how these cases are decided, it is clear that copyright enforcement will become more difficult in the coming years. One solution that has been suggested is to increase the amount of information in the public domain through an increase in government subsidies for information creation.

Federal Subsidies

The federal government already subsidizes the creation of certain information. It does so either directly, through the activity of government agencies and the award of grants and contracts to private organizations or individuals, or indirectly, through regulation and the establishment of certain tax benefits or other preferential treatment.

Census data, economic statistics and weather data are examples of information that the government collects and distributes directly. In addition, the government sponsors research and data collection by private individuals, provides indirect subsidies through some forms of regulation (the licensing of broadcasters to use the radio spectrum, for example), and administers tax laws that provide significant incentives for corporations to invest in research and development.

Government subsidies could provide one way to avoid some of the problems that are found in copyright and patent protections. They could guarantee payment to the creator of the information, while eliminating the need for the complex legal structure that now governs copyright. There is, however, a danger that government subsidy could result in government manipulation of the content of the information. Clearly, that would be in opposition to the principle of diversity of information, both in source and content.

Most observers feel that a continuation of a mixed approach is the wisest, though probably not the easiest, course of action. There is a place for government subsidy, but there is also the need for copyright and patent law to protect the creator of information working outside the purview of the government.

INFORMATION MARKETS

Information markets are not like other commodity markets. One reason for this is that information products act differently from typical commodities such as shoes or corn. As a result, information markets breed new policy questions at an alarming rate. These issues may be broken into two categories: issues relevant to federal regulation of information markets and industries, and issues concerning competition between public and private sector organizations.

Defining Information as a Product

Although it has become commonplace to speak of practically everyone as being in the "information business" and to describe our era as the "information age," information remains difficult to define. A review of its distinguishing characteristics may, however, be helpful. Information is different from other commodities in the following ways:

• Possession. It can be possessed by many people at the same time;

• Exclusion. Because of the simultaneity of possession, exclusion is difficult if not impossible. Once information is sold, other, non-paying, individuals may also possess it or benefit from it;

• Transferral. It is difficult to establish the value of information without revealing the information itself. Unlike automobiles, once the information is described, it is essentially transferred;

• Depletion. Information cannot be used up or worn out, although it can become obsolete; and

• Division. Although commodities containing information may be divided into units (books are an example), information itself is difficult to divide. Ideas and information are often interrelated in complex, poorly defined units.[12]

Inefficiencies in Information Markets

Because of these differences, information markets based on traditional models tend to be economically inefficient. Many of the inefficiencies in information markets stem from the following conditions and characteristics:

• Information production and distribution often tend toward economies of scale and scope; that is, larger firms tend to operate at lower unit costs, whether producing a single product, in the case of economies of scale, or a variety of products, in the case of economies of scope;

• There can be structural and pricing barriers to the entry of information firms into the market. In some cases, regulation forecloses entry of new firms. For example, the regulation of existing telephone companies as *de facto* monopolies for the provision of telephone lines has, at times, foreclosed the entry of other companies into this market; and

• The government's enforcement of anti-trust laws seeks to break up anti-competitive market structures and pricing arrangements and encourages competition, but the government itself can create inefficiencies if it arbitrarily divides up markets.[13]

Through these inefficiencies, information markets often fail to encourage free competition, which is assumed to promote diversity of information. When this happens, many of the social and political values stemming from the free flow of ideas may be threatened.

Regulating Ownership

Policies regulating information industries and information markets are meant to accomplish two objectives: 1) maintain diversity and 2) ensure the equitable distribution of information goods and services. To achieve the first objective, regulations are established that prohibit monopolies. To achieve the second objective, regulations are sometimes established to permit the growth of monopolies (such as the regulations that permitted AT&T to gain a monopoly over the nation's telephone system).

There are two types of regulatory policies designed to ensure diversity of viewpoint. The first set of policies promotes ownership of media outlets by ethnic, political or religious minorities. Some of these policies provide "preference in hearing license applications, and greater availability of loan funds to minority enterprises."[14] The second set of policies restricts the number of media outlets that any one individual or group may own.

Despite these ownership restrictions, large and powerful organizations have come to dominate the nation's information and entertainment industries. In this instance, economies of scale do not appear to work to the best interests of the public. Diversity of viewpoint is imperiled when access to news and information is controlled by a few.

Regulated Monopolies

In contrast to policies that promote competition, there are also government policies designed to restrict competition in order to achieve equity in the distribution of information. The postal service and AT&T are examples of monopolies created through this type of government intervention. In these instances, practices such as price discrimination and cross-subsidies, which would be prohibited in a freely competitive environment, are encouraged. These practices make it possible for the postal service and the telephone company to provide services to individuals living in areas in which service would be unprofitable or prohibitively expensive from a competitive point of view. In addition, other companies are prohibited from "cream skimming" (the practice of serving only the profitable markets, leaving the unprofitable markets to the regulated monopoly). In theory, this also allows regulated monopolies to use income from high-use, low-cost markets to subsidize services to individuals in low-use, high-cost markets.

Information Policy and AT&T

The 1982 consent decree governing the breakup of AT&T (the largest corporation in the world) marked a shift in federal policy toward regulated monopolies. Actually, while the division of AT&T into new corporate structures is a dramatic new step, it is a move consistent with policy trends of the last 20 years. With the emergence of increasingly sophisticated computer and communications technologies, the Federal Communications Commission has slowly permitted companies to compete with AT&T in the provision of telephone equipment and long-distance service. Under the 1982 decision, AT&T will be allowed to compete in unregulated product and service markets through a separate subsidiary (later named American Bell). In return, AT&T will be required to divest itself of its 23 "regional operating companies"—the companies that provide local telephone service. However, AT&T will be allowed to retain control of the Bell System's long-distance lines.

Some observers fear that this move will not be in the public interest. Consumer advocates predict rising local telephone rates (which had previously been subsidized by long-distance rates), the inability of the government to adequately monitor the division between regulated and unregulated activities, and danger to the smaller firms with whom AT&T will be competing. There is some fear that competition with a previously protected company, which operated with revenues that exceeded the gross national products of many nations, is in fact no competition at all. On the other hand, proponents of the plan forecast greater diversity for the consumer and a reduced regulatory responsibility for the federal government. Developments will no doubt be monitored closely by individuals representing both points of view.

Public Sector/Private Sector Competition

In addition to intervening in the information marketplace through regulatory activities, the federal government is also said to intervene when it acts as a competitor to other information providers. Charges that the federal government acts as an unfair competitor in the information marketplace have proliferated in recent years. As previously discussed, almost every information distribution activity of the federal government has come under attack.

NCLIS Report

In the library world, debate on the appropriate relationship between the public and private sectors with respect to information distribution was fueled by the publication in 1982 of the NCLIS report, *Public Sector/Private Sector Interaction in Providing Information Services.* This controversial and sometimes contradictory document affirms:

> On the one hand government clearly has responsibilities for information functions in collection and distribution of information in areas defined by the Constitution and mandated by Congress. At the very least, there is information that government must provide—a record of its actions, explanations of the law, descriptions of services. On the other hand, as the government's role

in producing and providing information expands, the likelihood increases that the greater diversity achievable by private investment will be discouraged.

To resolve this dilemma the report recommends: "The federal government should not provide information products and services in commerce except when there are compelling reasons to do so, and then only when it protects the private sector's every opportunity to assume the function(s) commercially."

On the face of it, there appears to be a conflict in values here. On the one hand, the government is charged with providing access to information by and about the government. On the other hand, it is responsible for maintaining the diversity of thought and viewpoint achievable through a "marketplace of ideas." Some might interpret this as a conflict between individual rights and property rights.

If that is the case, several questions arise. Whose property is government-produced information? When does distribution become competition? Under what circumstances is the federal government justified in intervening in the information market? Is there a hierarchy of values that would be useful in resolving these issues?

Perhaps the most striking aspect of the NCLIS recommendations is the manner in which they conflict with trends in information policy over the past 20 years, trends that assumed that the federal government should provide information to the public unless there was a compelling reason *not* to do so. The reversal of this assumption appears to place the economic good of private corporations above the social, political and economic good of individual citizens.

Public vs. Private Interests

If property rights are seen as paramount in a specific case, an analysis of the property itself becomes relevant. As noted above, information behaves quite differently from other commodities. Moreover, it is a widely held belief that ownership of information resides with the creator of that information. In discussions regarding the government role in the information marketplace, no one has suggested that the federal government refrain from creating information, only that it refrain from distributing it. It remains unclear why the government should relinquish ownership of information produced with tax dollars, or why it should withhold information it has produced.

Many argue that the private companies should distribute government-produced information because they can distribute it more cheaply, because they add value by their handling of the information, and because they ensure diversity in the means of distribution and dissemination. Yet there is no compelling evidence that the private sector is any more or less efficient than the public sector. There are examples of waste and mismanagement in both, and the range of efficiency is wide in each.

It is clear, however, that the public sector and the private sector have different goals that may result in apparent differences in efficiency. While private corporations are primarily concerned with making a profit, the government is primarily concerned with providing services that are in the public interest (even though they may not be profitable).

When dealing with information, there are situations in which a corporation may successfully take government-produced information, repackage it in a more attractive format and turn a profit. In doing this, however, it skims off the profitable information product and leaves the information that is in less demand. This suggests that distribution of government-produced information by the private sector may actually result in a decrease in diversity since, unlike most private companies, the government would tend to reinvest revenues from its more profitable information services to support important, but less profitable, services.

Fair vs. Unfair Competition

"Competition" has become a banner word in discussions of the relationships between the public and private sectors. Generally, competition in the marketplace is assumed to be good, while intervention by the government is assumed to be unfair and therefore bad. The 1982 NCLIS report lists examples of government information services that some consider unfairly competitive with private sector offerings. They include: the Worldwide Information & Trade System, the National Library of Medicine, ERIC, the online indexing service developed by the National Institute of Mental Health, the Congressional Research Service, the Library of Congress's SCORPIO System, LEGIS (the Congressional Legislative Information Service), the Government Printing Office, NTIS, the online data base service established by the Department of Energy, the Census Bureau's information services, and the National Standard Reference Data System.

Actually, almost everything the government does could be construed as competitive with the private sector in one way or another. Public schools compete with private schools. Public health services compete with private physicians. Police compete with private security services. Libraries compete with book stores. Few would suggest that the government abandon its responsibility in these important areas. The government intervenes, competes if you will, to protect certain social values.

Social Values and Responsibilities

In the information marketplace, there are important social values at risk as well. The first principle governing information produced by and about the federal government is that it should be made available to all citizens wishing it unless there is a compelling reason for limiting access. (These limitations were described earlier in this chapter.) The second principle guides government intervention in the marketplace of privately produced information. It maintains that the government should seek and promote diversity of thought and equity in distribution.

In spite of these principles, the trend in the early 1980s has been away from protection of an individual's right to know. Although the argument that the federal government is an unfair competitor is specious, it continues to be used as an excuse to relieve the government of its responsibility for disseminating and providing access to a wide range of information.

INFORMATION MANAGEMENT

For the federal government, information management issues are issues related to the efficiency and effectiveness of information handling within the government itself. Federal information management issues have received considerable attention in recent years, chiefly because of the large expenditures of money involved. For example, estimated federal expenditures for data processing alone amounted to $6 billion in FY 1981. In 1977 the Commission on Federal Paperwork (CFPW) estimated that the federal government spends from $25 to $30 billion a year on data collection and paperwork.[15]

In spite of the government's massive expenditures on data processing, problems of information management continue. They include: information glut and information scarcity, information redundancy, faulty information, unreasonable information collection and reporting burdens, and excessive costs of handling information within an agency or organization.[16]

Through laws and regulations, the government has established a number of policies designed to deal with these problems. The most significant policies are contained in the following: the Federal Reports Act, the Federal Records Act, the Brooks Act, the Privacy Act, the Freedom of Information and Paperwork Reduction Acts (both of which were discussed earlier) and OMB Circular No. A-76. Of these, the Paperwork Reduction Act has been the most sweeping in its overall impact and in the many ways it has modified, clarified or replaced provisions of other legislation.

Federal Reports Act

The Federal Reports Act of 1942 was the first government-wide attempt to limit redundancy in the collection of data by government agencies and to reduce the paperwork burden for private citizens and corporations. This legislation authorized the Office of Management and Budget to review the reporting forms of federal agencies, to investigate the need for information and to designate one agency as the sole collector of data required by two or more agencies. Although powers conferred by this legislation are broad, their implementation has been limited. The questionable effectiveness of this legislation, together with the introduction of new technologies and management techniques, led the Commission on Federal Paperwork to make a number of recommendations, many of which were incorporated into the Paperwork Reduction Act of 1980.

Federal Records Act

The Federal Records Act (1950) governs the federal archives and empowers the National Archives and Record Service (NARS) to improve the creation, maintenance and use of records by federal agencies. The major problem with this legislation has been the jurisdictional conflict generated between NARS (which administers the Federal Records Act) and OMB (which administers the Federal Reports Act). The primary point of contention flows from the failure to define "record" and "report." The Paperwork Reduction Act clearly shifted power away from NARS and toward OMB as the lead agency of the federal government with respect to management of all paperwork. It does, however, leave the management of official records in the hands of NARS.

Brooks Act

The original intent of the Brooks Act was to provide for the efficient procurement of automated data-processing and telecommunications equipment in the federal government. Passed in 1965, the Act spreads responsibility for oversight, standard setting and decision making among three federal agencies: OMB, the National Bureau of Standards within the Department of Commerce, and the General Services Administration. Instead of promoting efficiency and competition, however, the provisions of the bill actually served to diminish competition in procurement. The Paperwork Reduction Act has replaced this distributed pattern promoted by the Brooks Act with a centralized one. Primary responsibility for automated data processing procurement and management is now vested with the new Information Policy Office in OMB.

Privacy Act and Freedom of Information Act

The Privacy Act and the Freedom of Information Act are discussed in earlier sections of this chapter. While designed to protect basic individual rights and freedoms, they also have implications for the internal information management of the federal government.

Paperwork Reduction Act

As noted above, the most sweeping of the laws concerning information management is the Paperwork Reduction Act of 1980. The purpose of this legislation, as described earlier in the chapter, is to improve the efficiency of federal information management. To summarize, the Act consolidates control over all federal government paperwork in one central office located in OMB; it establishes tests governing requests for information collection and distribution; and it establishes a federal information locator system to avoid duplication of effort. The Act mandated a goal of 25% reduction of paperwork burden over three years, and it combined the following functions in OMB: general information, paperwork clearance, statistical policy, records management, privacy, automatic data processing and telecommunications.

As the Act was implemented, a number of new questions were raised. Is it really wise to centralize so much power in the hands of so few? Is efficiency really the primary goal of government? How are conflicts between information access policies and information management policies to be resolved?

Office of Management and Budget Circular No. A-76

A final federal policy concerning information management is contained in OMB Circular No. A-76, Performance of Commercial Activities. Originally issued in 1955, this policy became controversial in 1983 when proposed revisions were published that would change the manner in which the federal government handles its own libraries and information centers.

A-76 is based on the stated policy that "the government should not compete with its citizens" and that it is "the general policy of the government to rely on competitive private enterprise to supply the products and services it needs." If proposed changes in regulations are adopted, they will result in federal library services being contracted to private companies much more frequently than is now the case.

Those opposing the new regulations feel that this policy will have a long-term negative impact on federal libraries and their ability to provide adequate services. Several analysts note that the criteria for cost measurement are different for federal agencies and private vendors. Others object to the "deprofessionalization" that is likely to result from the substitution of lower-paid employees for professional librarians. Still others feel that proposed regulations leave the government without necessary protections and that service is likely to deteriorate.

Like the Paperwork Reduction Act, the revised version of Circular A-76 appears to flow from a confused set of goals. Under the current interpretation of the circular, economic efficiency would be given priority over quality of service. If federal libraries are in fact downgraded, it will mark the first time in the history of this nation that the federal government has turned away from its commitment to promoting informed decision making.

INTERNATIONAL INFORMATION POLICY ISSUES

Although the focus of this chapter is the federal role in domestic information policy, new communications technologies (particularly satellite technologies) have made it increasingly difficult for any nation to remain isolated from international information policy issues. For the United States, the key question seems to be the extent to which the federal government should base its position in international dealings on the principles that govern domestic information policy. Even though many of the issues that dominate discussions of international information policy seem similar to the issues discussed in this chapter (access to information, ownership and copyright, etc.), the international context suggests the possibility of different solutions.

In the international arena, for example, the United States commitment to freedom of information must be balanced against national security and other concerns. Although a complete discussion of international information policy issues is beyond the scope of this book, the following examples suggest the size and scope of the questions involved:

• The telephone and message service industries in the United States are becoming increasingly competitive, and their partial or complete deregulation may be just over the horizon. As United States' services interconnect with government owned and operated facilities in other nations, significant questions arise about such matters as pricing policies and definitions of universal service;

• As U.S. data bases become increasingly accessible to users in other countries, questions arise about the sharing of information generated or subsidized by the federal government, particularly when there are no reciprocal requirements for other countries;

• The knotty problems of United States copyright law, particularly regarding consent for copying and eligibility of a work for copyright, take on new dimensions as electronic systems speed creative works of Americans to consumers in all corners of the world; and

• The domestic conflict that has arisen between privacy protection for personal information and open availability of information becomes even more complex as personal information is regularly transmitted across national boundaries.[17]

These and a host of other issues will be addressed through discussions, conferences and treaties. The specific resolutions espoused by the United States will no doubt reflect the principles articulated in domestic information policies.

LIBRARY PLANNING AND POLICY MAKING

The information policies and practices described above have a real and continuing impact on libraries. There is another group of federal policies, however, that are more directly related to libraries and library development. This section examines those policies and activities, and considers how federal library planning and policy making has shaped the growth and development of library services.

Most planning and policy making for libraries takes place as an integral part of the federal functions described in preceding chapters—grants-in-aid, research and development, and data collection and distribution. In this respect, the primary planning and policy-making agencies are those that have money to give or programs to implement. Planning and policy issues for these agencies seem fairly straightforward. How much and to whom should money be distributed? What type of research and demonstration activity should be funded? What are the most effective mechanisms for federal data collection and distribution?

The manner in which library planning and policy making takes place can best be described by looking at two federal agencies engaged in library planning activities: the Department of Education (Library Programs Division) and the National Commission on Libraries and Information Science. The first is responsible for grants-in-aid and some research efforts, while the second serves as an advisory agency, responsible quite specifically for planning and policy making.

Department of Education, Library Programs Division

Chapters 4 and 5 described the activities of the Library Programs Division (formerly the Office of Libraries and Learning Technologies) in the Department of Education. Although it is responsible for administering most of the major library grants-in-aid programs, LPD is not just a funding agency. In order to properly administer its grants-in-aid programs, LPD must develop regulations governing distribution of funds, and these regulations have the force of law. In particular, the regulations developed during the administration of the Library Services and Construction Act (LSCA) and the Higher Education Act (HEA) have had a major impact on library development nationwide. Moreover, three characteristics of LSCA and HEA give LPD a great deal of added influence:

1. LSCA and HEA provide the major portion of federal grants to libraries;

2. The grants are distributed widely to libraries throughout the country; and

3. The acts incorporate legislative and regulatory requirements that can effect change far beyond the amount of money involved.

Reward and Punishment

For any policy to be effective, there must be some compelling incentives for individuals to assent to its provisions. The most common incentive is fear of punishment for non-compliance. Most legislative acts include provisions for punishing violators, and regulatory agencies are usually empowered to levy sanctions against those guilty of non-compliance.

The alternative type of incentive provides rewards for compliance. Under this system, money is usually distributed to agencies and organizations on the basis of how completely they comply with regulations and grant guidelines.

Impact of LPD Policies

Because LPD is really the only game in town as far as libraries go, and because so many libraries are beneficiaries of the programs administered by the Division, LPD regulations have a far-reaching effect. The most obvious example of LPD's influence is the requirement that states have a state library agency and a state plan to receive federal LSCA monies. This one requirement has promoted the growth and development of state library agencies throughout the country, and it has resulted in a corresponding expansion of the state role in supporting local libraries.

Although the requirement itself was a federal action, it is important to note that the effect was to push the responsibility for planning down to the state and local levels. Thus, in this instance, the federal government did not try to establish a unified approach to library development nationwide. Instead, it required planning at the point of service. Although this policy has resulted in some unevenness of service from state to state, it has also created a great deal more commitment on the part of those who must turn the federal plan into reality. A more extensive discussion of this subject is found in Chapter 4.

National Commission on Libraries and Information Science

Unlike LPD, whose primary purpose is to administer grants-in-aid, the National Commission on Libraries and Information Science (NCLIS) has been established for the specific purpose of planning and policy making. Created in 1970 through Public Law 91-345, the Commission has

> . . . the primary responsibility for developing or recommending overall plans
> for, and advising the appropriate governments and agencies on, the policy . . .

that library and information services adequate to meet the needs of the people of the United States are essential to achieve national goals and to utilize most effectively the nation's educational resources and that the federal government will cooperate with state and local governments and public and private agencies in assuring optimum provision of such services.[18]

To achieve this objective, NCLIS is authorized to:

1. Advise the President and the Congress on the implementation of national policy;

2. Conduct studies, surveys, and analyses of the library and informational needs of the nation, and the means by which these needs may be met;

3. Appraise the adequacies and deficiencies of current library and information resources and services and evaluate the effectiveness of current library and information science programs;

4. Develop overall plans for meeting national library and informational needs and for the coordination of activities at the federal, state and local levels;

5. Advise federal, state, local, and private agencies regarding library and information sciences;

6. Promote research and development activities;

7. Submit to the President and the Congress a report on its activities during the preceding fiscal year; and

8. Make and publish such additional reports as it deems to be necessary.

Commission Activities

Under this broad mandate, NCLIS has conducted hearings, established task forces and produced numerous reports concerning various aspects of nationwide library development. Most notable is the Commission's program document, *Toward a National Program for Library and Information Services: Goals for Action,* published in 1975 after an extended series of public hearings. According to the document, major federal responsibilities are to:

1. Encourage and promulgate standards, including standards for: computer software, access and security protocols, data elements and codes; bibliographic formats, film, computer tapes and sound recordings; literary texts in machine-readable form; and reprography and micrographics;

2. Make unique and major resource collections available nationwide by providing incremental funding to institutions with unique resources of national significance such as the Harvard University Libraries and the New York Public Library;

3. Develop centralized services for networking. Examples include: a national audio-visual repository, a national system of interlibrary communication, a national depository for the preservation of microform masters, and a national periodicals bank;

4. Explore computer use;

5. Apply new forms of telecommunications;

6. Support research and development; and

7. Foster cooperation with similar national and international programs.

The 1975 NCLIS document also recommends increased responsibilities for the Library of Congress, including: 1) expansion of its lending function to that of a National Lending Library of final resort; 2) expansion of coverage under the National Program for Acquisitions and Cataloging; 3) expansion of MAchine-Readable Cataloging (MARC); 4) the online distribution of the bibliographic data base to the various nodes of the national network; 5) an augmented reference service to support the national system for bibliographic service; 6) operation of a comprehensive National Serials Service; 7) establishment of a technical services center to provide training in, and information about, Library of Congress techniques and processes, with emphasis on automation; 8) development of improved access to state and local government publications; and 9) further implementation of the National Program to preserve physically deteriorating library materials.

Impact of Commission Activities

The exact impact of NCLIS planning and policy making is difficult to evaluate. There are rarely any immediate results, because NCLIS has neither the carrot of funding nor the stick of regulatory authority needed to make recommendations stick. Moreover, NCLIS has historically been funded at such a low level that many of its resources are used simply to continue its own existence.

One of the continuing anomalies of the federal government is that a small agency such as NCLIS has the same reporting responsibilities as a large agency like the Department of Education. As a result, NCLIS has never really received the "critical mass" of funding that would permit it to commit a significant percentage of its funding to program-related activities.

Even if NCLIS were funded at an adequate level, the concept of centralized planning probably needs to be reexamined. Few of the recommendations made by NCLIS have been implemented on a broad scale. Some, such as the notion that networking should be centralized, have been bypassed by time and technology. Others, such as the establishment of a National Periodicals Center (NPC), have been met with outright hostility. In the case of the NPC, a large investment of time and effort resulted in a Pyrrhic victory: legislation enacted with a triggering mechanism that almost guarantees it will never become operative.

In spite of these limitations, NCLIS has provided a neutral ground for the discussion of important topics. As a small organization with minimum funding and maximum visibility, NCLIS can help focus attention on the issues of the day. It cannot provide financial assistance like the Library Programs Division, it cannot conduct research and development like the Library of Congress, and it does not actually produce data bases like the National Library of Medicine. Its job is planning and policy making, a job that it can accomplish only through negotiation and consensus building.

CONCLUSION

The term "national information policy" evokes emotional responses that vary from person to person. To some, a national information policy is a unified, consistent set of guidelines governing information-handling activities at the national level. To others, it is a catch-all phrase that has lost its meaning in a diffusion of interpretations.

Politics and Power

Whether one sees national information policy as a policy or as a set of policies, it is clear that two key elements are involved: politics and the distribution of power. Although many feel that the Reagan administration has exhibited little interest in the subject of information policy, a careful examination of decisions made regarding information collection and distribution reveals a series of decisions that are consistent in their goal of shifting power and control from the public to the private sector.

Public vs. Private Sector

Increasingly, all of the issues grouped under the umbrella of "information policy" can be seen as questions in the same debate—the continuing debate between the public and private sectors over the role each should play in the collection and distribution of information. These issues permeate the continuing saga of AT&T as it fights its way through the courts and the Congress. They can be seen in the recent suggestion that NTIS should be dismantled and that federal libraries should be contracted to private firms. They are also an underlying element in the Reagan administration's restrictive interpretations of the Freedom of Information Act, and they provided the underlying rationale for the enactment and subsequent implementation of the Paperwork Reduction Act.

Information Policy and Library Policy

In many ways, information policy and library policy are indistinguishable. Information policies govern the content of information available to individuals, the manner in which that information may be acquired and distributed, and the subsequent use of the information. Political justification for the very existence of libraries rests on the strong presumption that individuals must have access to information by and about the government if they are to participate effectively in the political process. Social justification for libraries rests on the presumption that diversity of opinion enriches all aspects of our lives and leads to progress. Economic justification for libraries rests on the presumption that information leads to more effective decision making, for an economy founded on true "free market" principles presumes an informed consumer population.

Specific federal policy issues that relate to the functioning of libraries include: the availability of government information, the continuation and scope of depository libraries, the interpretation of the Freedom of Information Act, the definition of obscenity, the extent to which library records are considered private, the continued operation of NTIS, the A-76 regulations as they apply to the operation of federal libraries, and the interpretation and application of the Paperwork Reduction Act.

Library planning and policy-making efforts undertaken by federal agencies take place in an environment that is already conditioned by policies established by the courts, the Congress and the executive branch. Movement in the early 1980s has clearly been toward a more restricted flow of information. At a time when we seem to be drowning in a flood of information, it is easy to overlook the fact that the flow of information from the federal government has diminished and that the springs that supply needed information have begun to dry up.

FOOTNOTES

1. Lawrence S. Robertson and Robert J. Aldrich, "Dissemination of Information" in *Issues in Information Policy* (Washington, DC: U.S. Department of Commerce, 1981).

2. *Ibid.*

3. Marilyn Killebrew Gell, "The Ministry of Truth," *Library Journal* 106:399 (February 15, 1981).

4. *Ibid.*

5. Louis Harris & Associates and Dr. Alan F. Westin, *The Dimensions of Privacy: A National Opinion Research Survey of Attitudes Toward Privacy* (Stevens Point, WI: Sentry Insurance, 1979).

6. Robert R. Belair, "Information Privacy" in *Issues in Information Policy* (Washington, DC: U.S. Department of Commerce, 1981).

7. *Ibid.*

8. *Ibid.*

9. *Ibid.*

10. Arthur A. Bushkin and Jane H. Yurow, *The Foundations of United States Information Policy* (Washington, DC: U.S. Department of Commerce, 1980).

11. David Y. Peyton, "The Creation of Information: Property Rights and Subsidies" in *Issues in Information Policy* (Washington, DC: U.S. Department of Commerce, 1981).

12. Yale M. Braunstein, "Information as a Commodity: Public Policy Issues and Recent Research" in *Information Services: Economics, Management, and Technology,* ed. by Robert M. Mason and John E. Creps, Jr. (Boulder, CO: Westview Press, 1981).

13. Arthur A. Bushkin and Jane H. Yurow, op. cit.

14. Lawrence S. Robertson and Robert F. Aldrich, op. cit.

15. Jane H. Yurow, Aaron B. Wildavsky and Stanley Pogrow, "Managing Information" in *Issues in Information Policy* (Washington, DC: U.S. Department of Commerce, 1981).

16. Arthur A. Bushkin and Jane H. Yurow, op. cit.

17. *Ibid.*

18. P.L. 91-345.

7
Library Networks

Any complete discussion of the federal role in library and information services must consider the growth and impact of library networks. In recent years, as the volume of information has grown, so has the need for library cooperation and resource sharing. At the same time, technical developments have provided the means for sophisticated levels of interlibrary communication. The convergence of these trends in the 1970s triggered an explosion of library network activities—an explosion that has already changed the nature of library services, and that may render libraries as we know them obsolete by the year 2000.

Although the federal government was not the initial sponsor or even the primary supporter of library networking, federal agencies have played an important role in network development. This chapter will define library and information networks, and briefly describe the history of network activities to date. It will also examine how political, economic and technological conditions have influenced federal contributions to network development, and how the federal government might make a positive contribution to shaping and supporting future resource-sharing activities.

DEFINITIONS

The word "network" has been variously defined. Some use the term in a general way to mean "a group of individuals or organizations that are interconnected."[1] This definition encompasses all types of cooperative activities among libraries, including formal and informal library consortia, information retrieval systems and groups of library users having common interests.

Under this broad definition, the beginning of library networks would coincide with the beginning of library cooperation—a movement that is said to have started in 1853, when Charles Jewett suggested the use of stereotype plates to produce a national union catalog. Other landmarks on the long and difficult road of library cooperation include the initiation of the Library of Congress's catalog card production and distribution service in 1901, and the development of the LC book catalog and the National Union Catalog (both of which existed by 1950).

While this very broad definition of "library network" is still used by some, a more precise term is gaining general acceptance. Today, the term "network" is frequently used to mean "both the organizations and systems that link libraries together via telecommunications with computer-controlled message switching and data-base access."[2] Characteristics include:

• Support derived primarily from payment for services from participating libraries;

• Full time staff;

• Control by an independent governing body with a high level of involvement (generally through a board of directors from participating libraries);

• Built around a cooperatively maintained bibliographic data base in machine-readable form;

• Linked online by a telecommunications system.[3]

This relatively narrow definition excludes cooperatives and consortia that are not organized around computer and communications systems. Although many of these organizations are becoming increasingly involved in networking activities, the distinction is important to make in the context of emerging issues.

EVOLUTION OF LIBRARY NETWORKS

Library networks are a product of the times. They are the natural consequence of political, economic and technological trends that affect all aspects of our society. More specifically, library networks are the result of economic constraints, technological imperatives and the need to access a vast and growing body of print and non-print materials.

There was a time when scholarly libraries attempted to acquire all published materials in specific subject areas. Those days are now gone. In the United States alone, approximately 40,000 books are published each year, and worldwide publication of periodicals is estimated to be around 120,000 titles per year. In addition, research libraries must select from among numerous serials, foreign publications and government documents. Faced with this explosion of information, libraries can no longer hope to meet the needs of their clients using only the materials from their own collections.

Even if it were physically possible to collect all publications, such a task has become an economic daydream. The economic picture in recent years has been gloomy. For most libraries, inflation and the declining fiscal capacity at all levels of government have resulted in a double problem: increased costs and reduced budgets. Libraries have struggled to do more with less, and most have scrambled to find new ways to increase their productivity.

Significantly, while labor and materials costs have risen sharply, the costs of computer and communications capabilities have decreased. As a result, many library administrators have turned to information technology to help reduce costs, increase productivity and improve access to materials owned by other institutions.

As mentioned above, although recent technological developments have fueled a rapid growth in network activities, the concept of library networks grew out of a tradition of library cooperation that dates from the 19th century. While a full history of those early cooperative efforts is outside the scope of this book, most were based on the belief that intellectual effort profits from the sharing of resources. The first major attempt to describe a library network, Norman Meise's *Conceptual Design of an Automated National Library System,* did not appear until 1969.[4] In the design, Meise described the potential of information technology and its possible applications for strengthening cooperative interrelationships among libraries.

Conference on Interlibrary Communications and Information Networks

In 1970 the Conference on Interlibrary Communications and Information Networks laid the philosophical groundwork for the development of library networks. The conference was sponsored by the U.S. Office of Education and the American Library Association, and it was held at Airlie House in Warrenton, VA. Conference participants predicted that "networks will bring drastic changes to administrative relationships among existing institutions, and that new agencies are likely to be created to meet the pressures of networking potential and capabilities."[5]

It was also noted at that conference that the idea of a "National Library Network," complete with federal funding and national planning and management, was born. Some of the basic tenets professed at the conference include:

• That national planning, leadership and direction are essential to network development;

• That large-scale federal funding of library networks is essential to their development;

• That networks will result from a linkage of local and state networks and will build upon present state-level cooperatives and consortia (such as the New York NYSILL interlibrary loan networks) and from local academic networks based on local university computer centers; and

• That some type of national agency, such as NCLIS, Library of Congress, or a new federal agency, will be required to govern and manage the development of a national library network.[6]

In the decade that has elapsed since these preconditions were articulated, networking activity has grown far beyond the wildest dreams of the participants. By 1982, 25 network organizations were serving more than 3500 institutions through more than 5500 online terminals. Contrary to what the conference participants had expected, this rapid growth has occurred not as a direct result of federal funding or leadership, but through local initiative and self-financing.

The MARC System and the Birth of OCLC

The pivotal event that led to the emergence of an unplanned and uncoordinated system of networks was an action taken by the Library of Congress in the 1960s. At that time, LC embarked on the creation of machine-readable cataloging data. In 1969 the Library began distributing the data on computer tape. MARC tapes (as they came to be known) provided a standard, but LC made no provision for providing direct, online access to the MARC data base. As a result, many library organizations experimented with various uses and applications of the tapes. One such organization was the Ohio College Library Center (now the Online Computer Library Center). OCLC devised a system through which MARC tapes, supplemented by cataloging done by member libraries, could be used to generate catalog cards quickly and economically. In 1970 OCLC performed its first batch processing for member libraries, and in 1971 it became the first organization to offer online operations.

OCLC-Related Networks

The OCLC initiative sparked changes in a number of regional network activities. The New England Library Information Network (NELINET) abandoned its efforts to develop an independent data base and contracted for services with OCLC, as did the Pittsburgh Regional Library Center and the Five Associated University Libraries group. These actions established what was to become the dominant pattern for the 1970s. Through much of the decade, regional networks were formed "in order to facilitate contracting with OCLC for the use of its cataloging subsystem, to provide training and assistance in the use of the sub-system, and to provide a focal point for other network activities."[7]

This system of distributing OCLC services through state and regional networks worked so well that, in the period from 1971 to 1982, OCLC grew from a system providing online service to a single library through one terminal linked to a sole computer to a system serving 4490 terminals in more than 3000 libraries and requiring more than 30 mainframe and minicomputers.[8]

OTHER MAJOR NETWORKS

Although the vast majority of state and multistate networks were designed to broker the services of OCLC, a few chose to develop independent data bases and offer additional services. Included in this latter group are the Washington Library Network (WLN), the Research Libraries Information Network (RLIN) and the University of Toronto Library Automation System (UTLAS).

Washington Library Network

WLN, the youngest and smallest of the online networks, began formal operations in 1977. It is characterized by its affiliation with the Washington State Library, its emphasis on service to public libraries and its concentration on the development of replicable software. Because of its strong ties to the Washington State Library, WLN has never shown any inclination to compete with OCLC in the nationwide delivery of services, and it operates a continuing network system for libraries in the Pacific Northwest only. WLN has, however, invested more than $6 million in software development.[9] It currently provides not only an online cataloging capability, but also an acquisitions subsystem with fund accounting.

Rather than focus on building a large international data base, WLN has chosen to expand by licensing its software to local and regional organizations in the U.S. and other countries. Some observers feel that the WLN approach may be the wave of the future:

> As existing network organizations gain further organizational and financial maturity, and as the costs of computer hardware continue to decrease, replication of the WLN system, which would give them a greater measure of independence from OCLC and provide a system with different capabilities, appears to be an attractive alternative for many networks.[10]

Research Libraries Information Network

RLIN grew out of two separate developments: the Bibliographic Automation of Large Libraries using an Online Timesharing System (BALLOTS) network and the Research Libraries Group (RLG). Stanford University began BALLOTS in 1972, as a computerized cataloging service for its own library system. In 1975 the high cost of running the system led Stanford to make it more widely available. By 1978 more than 50 California libraries were using BALLOTS as a shared cataloging system, with 100 others using it to search for bibliographic data.

RLG was formed by Harvard, Yale, Columbia and the New York Public Library in 1974, as a means of achieving better services and improved quality control in large research libraries. Rather than develop its own software and network communications system, RLG decided in early 1978 to adopt the BALLOTS system. Stanford joined RLG later in 1978, and BALLOTS was reorganized to emphasize service to research libraries.

RLIN, as the reorganized system is now known, serves as the bibliographic data base and services arm of RLG. In addition to providing cataloging, acquisitions, fund accounting and serial control services, RLIN offers programs in the areas of preservation, shared collection development and management, and shared resources among the research libraries.

In spite of massive grants from the Carnegie, Dana, Hewlett, Mellon, Rockefeller and Sloan Foundations; a substantial, long-term loan from the Ford Foundation; and continuing support from the Council on Library Resources, the future of RLG is uncertain. Harvard University has dropped out of the group, many members maintain their memberships in other networks, and it is unclear whether RLG will be able to attract additional members without compromising on the quality of its service.

University of Toronto Library Automation Systems

UTLAS offers still another approach to networking. In 1959 the University of Toronto began converting its catalog records to machine-readable form. By the mid-1970s, it offered an online bibliographic system to a consortium of Canadian libraries. Currently, UTLAS is second in size to OCLC, and it is striving for an integrated, distributed network. UTLAS provides centralized data processing and locally operated systems, and it will run a user's file against MARC tapes, the Bibliothèque Nationale de Québec, the data base of the National Library of Canada and the National Library of Medicine. Moreover, its software can produce Computer-Output Microform (COM) catalogs, union lists, cards and tapes. In 1980 UTLAS acquired its first U.S. customer, the Rochester Institute of Technology.

CURRENT TRENDS AND DEVELOPMENTS

By the early 1980s, network activities in North America were dominated by the four major bibliographic utilities (OCLC, RLIN, UTLAS and WLN). Each was providing services to an established user base, and each was busy expanding and upgrading its services. As of July 1982, the four major networks were providing access to a combined total of more than 20 million bibliographic records, through 5605 installed user terminals.[11]

In spite of the apparent success that these numbers suggest, the major networks are showing signs of stress. The sheer size of the utilities has caused response delays and extended system downtime. In addition, competition is growing among the major utilities, as well as between the utilities and the regional networks. Finally, technological trends have begun to favor smaller, distributed systems.

Late in 1982, OCLC announced that it had copyrighted the format of its data base. Although this move was explained as a step necessary to protect the integrity of OCLC service, many regional networks felt that OCLC was attempting to squeeze them out of the networking market. Some observers maintain that the OCLC data base belongs to member libraries that generate the information, and many feel that the issue will ultimately be resolved in court.

While OCLC increases pressure on the regional networks, it is also stepping up its competition with WLN. WLN traditionally operates only as a regional network serving the Pacific Northwest. Its software could, however, provide significant competition to OCLC if it were aggressively marketed. Although WLN has previously refused to compete directly with OCLC, it is being forced to compete with OCLC Western for provision of regional service. Early in 1983, WLN began long-range planning that could result in a more vigorous marketing strategy.

As the size and cost of computer systems have decreased, a number of states and substate regions have moved to establish networks. Indiana Cooperative Library Services Authority (INCOLSA) was one of the first state networks, while networking efforts in Missouri and West Virginia are relatively recent.

Although state networks currently depend on the bibliographic utilities to perform some functions, it is not at all clear that this will be necessary in the future. Although some analysts see an ideal pattern of cooperation as one incorporating national, regional, state and local networks, such a pattern is unlikely. There appears to be far too much duplication of service to justify payments by individual libraries to multiple networks.

The primary threat to the continued dominance of OCLC as the chief bibliographic utility appears to be the potential development of a distributed system of state and/or regional networks. Although such a system is made possible by technological developments, it would still require access to a large data base and appropriate software. Thus, many observers feel that the increased competition between OCLC and WLN and the copyrighting of OCLC's data base format are OCLC's way of waging preemptive strikes against its potential competitors.

RELATIONSHIPS AMONG NETWORKS

Although the main subject of this chapter is the federal role in library networking, there are several important issues confronting networks that may not fall within the purview of the federal government. Most notable among these are issues concerning the relationships among networks. Until quite recently, many members of the library community assumed that network relationships had stabilized. OCLC served the country directly, RLIN met the needs of research libraries, and WLN remained a regional network with some very special software. In addition, regional service centers brokered the services of the larger networks and provided additional capabilities geared to the needs of their members.

Regional Service Centers

In the late 1970s, some observers began to wonder if the regional service centers had sufficient reason to continue their operations. Costs were rising, and there was an increasing need to develop some justification for charging fees considered by many to be too high. As these concerns were surfacing, SOLINET (Southeastern Library Network, Inc.), a regional broker for OCLC services, announced plans to adapt WLN software to its Burroughs equipment. Some analysts speculated about the potential impact on OCLC if SOLINET were to create a successful free-standing regional system.

Before the experiment was tried, however, the arrangement fell apart. For a variety of reasons, OCLC withdrew its offer to loan SOLINET money to support the experiment.

Shortly after the 1980 SOLINET announcement, NELINET announced a reduction in staff and a retrenchment in its plans for regional development in the New England area.

As mentioned earlier, while some regional networks appear to be floundering, library agencies in West Virginia and other states are beginning to explore the possibility of providing automated statewide networks. In addition to providing access to the major utilities, these networks would be able to incorporate a much higher degree of resource sharing through document delivery because of their geographic proximity.

The final outcome of these maneuverings is uncertain as of early 1983, but it is likely that, in the library world, the 1980s will be known as the decade of the great "networking wars."

State Library Networks

The statewide library networks appear to be in a strong position at this point for a number of reasons. First, current technology favors distributed systems. Except for a few services, such as shared cataloging, centralization seems to make little economic or technical sense. Second, state library agencies have grown in strength both politically and economically. While it is true that state agencies, like most other government agencies, are having a difficult time right now, they still have greater institutional strength than many of the regional networks. The pattern of federal support for the last 25 years has hastened their development, and they are now looking for expanded services. Finally, networking is ready to move into a new phase in which document delivery becomes more significant. For the next five to seven years, libraries are likely to continue to depend on interlibrary loans. Thus, systems that facilitate interlibrary loan will be more acceptable.

Continuing Issues

No matter what happens with statewide network development, the question of network relationships remains. How will the large utilities relate to each other; to the state, regional and local networks; and to individual libraries? What will happen to the regional service centers? How will technical issues such as the development of links between networks be resolved? Will relationships among networks be characterized by competition, cooperation or some combination of the two? To what extent will networking be centralized or decentralized?

Surrounding these issues is the larger question of federal involvement. What role, if any, should the federal government play in resolving issues arising from internetwork relationships? Although the government could act as a mediator or policy maker, there is no reason to expect that direct federal intervention would succeed. At this time, it seems more likely that the issues will be resolved in the marketplace.

FEDERAL ROLE IN DEVELOPING NETWORK ACTIVITIES

As the foregoing suggests, federal efforts in library networking have been deeply intertwined with the activities of other public and private groups. As a result, the exact role the federal government has played in promoting and shaping the development of existing library networks is difficult to discern. It is clear, however, that the role of the federal government has been vastly different from that envisioned at the 1970 Airlie House Conference. These differences and distinctions become even more apparent if we compare the preconditions presented at that conference with the following resolution on networking passed at the 1979 White House Conference on Library and Information Services:

WHEREAS, library and information services contribute significantly to information resources, and

WHEREAS, access to information and library resources available in all types of libraries is needed and must be equally available to all citizens, and

WHEREAS, all types of library and information centers have resources which can contribute to library and information services, networks, and programs at all geographic levels, and

WHEREAS, resource sharing is now mandated by the information explosion, the advance of modern technology, the rapidly escalating costs of needed resources, and the wide disparity between resources available to individuals by reason of geographic location or socio-economic position,

THEREFORE BE IT RESOLVED, that a comprehensive approach be taken to the planning and development of multitype library and information networks, including both profit and not-for-profit libraries from the public and private sector, and

BE IT FURTHER RESOLVED, that such plans be developed at the national, regional, and local level to include specific plans for a national periodicals system and the concept of a national lending library for print and nonprint materials, and

BE IT FURTHER RESOLVED, that plans be developed for the coordination of library and information networks and programs which would identify the responsibility for such coordination in the United States Department of Education's Office of Library and Learning Resources (or its successor) and the state library agencies, and such other agencies, organizations, or libraries as are involved in such networks, and

BE IT FURTHER RESOLVED, that control of such networks remain at the state or regional level, and

BE IT FURTHER RESOLVED, that mechanisms be developed to ensure access by all individuals to such networks and programs, and

BE IT FURTHER RESOLVED, that federal and state funds be made available to continue to support and interconnect existing networks, as well as to develop new networks, and that such funds be designated for network operations and for grants in support of local cooperative action, and

> BE IT FURTHER RESOLVED, that all agencies and institutions that pro-
> vide education and continuing education for library practitioners should
> offer training in the skills, knowledge, and abilities which will help ensure
> that practitioners are competent to provide access through these networks
> in a most effective manner.[12]

As the resolution indicates, the participants at the 1979 conference envisioned a far different role for the federal government in network development than that predicted by the participants at the Airlie House Conference. In place of centralized national planning, the 1979 resolution called for a comprehensive approach that would involve library agencies at the national, regional and local levels. Instead of "large-scale federal funding," both federal and state support were expected. Further, the requirement that a national agency "govern and manage the development of a national library network" was replaced by the resolution that "control of such networks remain at the state or regional level."

Federal Agency Involvement

Although most network activities started at the local and regional levels and grew "from the bottom up," two federal agencies have played key roles in shaping the direction of network development. Without the Library of Congress and the Office of Libraries and Learning Technologies (now the Library Programs Division), networks as we know them would not exist. The Library of Congress developed the MARC tapes, and then made the tapes available without centralized control or a predetermined prescription for how they should be used. The Office of Libraries and Learning Technologies provided support for libraries that was used to develop state and regional networks and to purchase bibliographic services provided by the utilities.

Research and Development

At the federal level, research and development continue at the Library of Congress and the National Library of Medicine. Similar research is supported in non-federal institutions by the National Science Foundation, the National Endowment for the Humanities and the Library Programs Division. LPD continues to be the only federal agency that provides financial aid that may be used for library operations. (For more information on federal research and grant programs, see Chapters 3, 4 and 5.)

Major data bases from which networks may draw information are provided by NLM and the National Agricultural Library, as well as by the Library of Congress. In addition, NLM and NAL operate actual networks, as does the Federal Library Committee.

FEDERAL ROLE IN NETWORK PLANNING AND POLICY MAKING

Planning and policy making is the specific mandate of the National Commission on Libraries and Information Science (NCLIS), but the Library of Congress and the Library Programs Division probably contribute significantly more to that effort. To a lesser extent, all of the federal agencies described above have some influence on planning and policy making. Any funding decision may be seen as a policy decision, and the creation of federal network systems that can be emulated is planning of a concrete type.

Of all the issues considered in this book, the most controversial by far is the federal role in planning and policy making. For many of those actually involved in library networking, the idea of a federally operated "national library network" seems to have fallen out of favor, if indeed it was ever in favor. Thus, the notions of a "national plan" or a "federal locus" appear in sharp contrast to the current reality of library networking.

Federal Planning vs. The Free Market

As mentioned earlier, networking activities have grown from the bottom up, reflecting the needs and struggles of local libraries and regional units. As a result, the bibliographic utilities and regional service centers incorporate an entrepreneurial spirit that appears to be more comfortable in a competitive environment than it is in a cooperative one.

Nevertheless, some cling to the notion that problems can be better solved in federal meeting rooms than in the open market. There is, however, little evidence to support this assertion. As Barbara Markuson puts it: "It is difficult to write of national-level network planning without being unduly critical."[13] Susan Martin takes a similar position:

> Now it appears that the concept of a nationwide network has indeed been overtaken by events. Simply stated, the bottom-up approach works better. The fact is that most librarians are not deeply involved in the development of a national bibliographic network. A large monolithic bibliographic network is no longer an objective useful to the goals of the North American library community. Rather, each library and each network continue to hold their own priorities, fitting into the nationwide jigsaw puzzle as appropriate.[14]

Although NCLIS, LC, NSF, LPD and other federal agencies have sponsored numerous reports and held countless planning meetings, it is not clear what these efforts have accomplished. To be sure, the federal government is capable of strong, centralized planning to achieve specific goals. But it does so only under one of three conditions:

1. It offers the carrot of financial support;
2. It carries the stick of federal regulation; or
3. It does it itself.

In the case of national network planning and policy making, none of these conditions prevail. Funding agencies are not charged with planning and policy making, and regulations with the power of enforcement are nonexistent. Agencies such as the Library of Congress that have "done it themselves" (with MARC, for instance) have generally been successful in their undertakings, but they have not attempted to set national standards or guidelines.

Planning and policy making in library networking is the function the federal government fulfills least well. To a large extent, the funding agencies are the most effective policy.

makers, for they can offer financial incentives for specific actions. But even they are limited. In addition, it is not at all clear that the library profession wants centralized planning for a set of services that are developing in response to local need. (For a more extensive discussion of the federal role in planning and policy making, see Chapter 6.)

Technical Standards

The single exception to the general resistance to federal intervention may be in the area of technical standards. Many observers feel that the establishment of federal hardware and software standards will at least not hinder the development of a nationwide network, and that such standards might even speed up the process. Even those who lack enthusiasm about general federal planning are often strongly supportive of a federal effort to establish technical standards:

> Whatever the shape of future national networking, technical compatibility is of prime importance; the development of standards for content representation, data communication and machine-to-machine communication must be stressed. If an agreed-upon goal is an integrated system which allows the same data to be used for a variety of functions, then the various parts of that system must accept the data without requiring extensive manipulation or rekeying.[15]

FUTURE FEDERAL ROLE

As this chapter has pointed out, networks are driven by technology and nourished in the political and economic climate of the times. Historically, they have been responsive not to a national directive, but to a local imperative. Social and economic trends serve to reinforce this trend toward locally funded and managed systems that require minimal intervention by the federal government. At the same time, technology is giving us smaller, faster and cheaper computing power. The dream of a computer in every library is much closer than we once believed possible. This is creating a situation in which local networks have not only a political and philosophical appeal, but an economic one as well. Further, as networks move beyond increasing productivity and providing bibliographic access to the actual delivery of information, the appeal of smaller systems will increase.

Critical Trends and Issues

The most critical set of networking issues will emerge in 10 to 20 years, as direct information service into homes becomes economically feasible and technologically efficient. What will the role of local libraries be when OCLC or some similar organization, using an interactive cable television channel, can provide electronic information directly to homes in a local library's service area? Perhaps the relationship of local libraries to the large utilities will come to resemble the relationship between network television stations and their local affiliates.

As networks continue to grow, libraries will become virtually indistinguishable from the networks supporting them. So far the federal role has been supportive, but nondirective. In spite of repeated statements that the federal government should be directing network development, that has not been the case, and it is probably a good thing.

In retrospect, the decision made by the Library of Congress to release the MARC tapes without specific directions as to their use appears to have been the best possible decision. This made experimentation possible, and today's networks are probably much stronger for it. So, too, federal grants-in-aid that were provided to state library agencies have helped ensure the continuing local locus of networking activities. These trends: local control, improved services, and economy and accountability are in harmony with the political climate of the times and are likely to be the determining factors for the future.

Goals of Federal Participation

In the future, the federal government should continue to support equal access to information for all citizens. This has, after all, been the goal of federal intervention since the Library Services Act sought to bring library service to the rural parts of the country.

Over the next few years, however, the means through which the federal government tries to achieve this goal may shift dramatically. Instead of striving for a centralized system in which some services are provided by federal agencies, federal support for a distributed system appears to make more sense. Also, instead of seeking a "locus of federal responsibility," the shared responsibility outlined in the White House Conference resolution might be a better objective.

Based on the information detailed in this chapter, it appears that some reasonable objectives for federal participation in library networking might be:

• Encourage the development of state and local networking capabilities by providing financial incentives for resource sharing;

• Encourage the continued participation of major research libraries by subsidizing resource development;

• Support research and development at an elevated level to achieve economies of scale, increased productivity, and advances in information technology (advances that might have a spillover effect on other parts of the economy);

• Promote use of the latest technology within the government itself, so federal agencies become a model for information handling and spin-off systems, much as the Library of Congress has already done;

• Provide a mechanism for the establishment and promulgation of technical standards; and

• Adopt a laissez-faire approach to the development of bibliographic utilities and state and regional networks, with the exception of support for R&D.

Under these objectives, the federal government would not be striving to be all things to all people, nor would it be seeking to develop a single monolithic structure. Instead, it would accept the somewhat messy approach to network development that has taken us very far very fast. In addition, it would recognize that some networks will succeed while others may fail, and that the multiple experiments are likely to give the library community a great many more options.

Thus, the appropriate roles of the federal government in network development are: innovator and manager of its own systems, supporter of research and development, promoter of local initiative and responsibility, subsidizer of collections of national resources, and facilitator in the development of standards.

FOOTNOTES

1. Susan K. Martin, *Library Networks, 1981-82* (White Plains, NY: Knowledge Industry Publications, Inc., 1981).

2. Barbara Evans Markuson and Blanche Woolls, eds., *Networks for Networkers* (New York: Neal-Schuman Publishers, 1980).

3. Norman D. Stevens, "Library Networks and Resource Sharing in the United States: An Historical and Philosophical Overview," *Journal of the American Society for Information Science* 31:405-413 (November 1980).

4. Norman R. Meise, *Conceptual Design of an Automated National Library System* (Metuchen, NJ: Scarecrow Press, 1969).

5. Joseph Becker, ed., *Proceedings of the Conference on Interlibrary Communications and Information Networks* (Chicago: American Library Association, 1971).

6. Barbara Evans Markuson, op. cit.

7. Norman D. Stevens, op. cit.

8. Joseph R. Matthews and Joan Frye Williams, "Bibliographic Utilities: Progress and Problems," *Library Technology Reports* 18:609-653 (November-December, 1982).

9. Barbara M. Robinson, "Cooperation and Competition among Library Networks," *Journal of the American Society for Information Science* 31:413-425 (November 1980).

10. Norman D. Stevens, op. cit.

11. Joseph R. Matthews, op. cit.

12. *Information for the 1980s: The Final Report of the White House Conference on Library and Information Services, 1979* (Washington, DC: Government Printing Office, 1980).

13. Barbara Evans Markuson, op. cit.

14. Susan K. Martin, op. cit.

15. *Ibid.*

8

The White House Conference on Library and Information Services

The 1979 White House Conference on Library and Information Services (WHCLIS) was probably the largest, most political event dealing with libraries that has yet taken place in this country. As such, it has special significance. This chapter will briefly describe the background and proceedings of WHCLIS, and then evaluate the conference from three perspectives: efficiency, effectiveness and relevancy.

First, the section on efficiency will consider how well WHCLIS worked as a conference, paying particular attention to questions concerning the best use of time and resources at the conference itself. Second, the section on effectiveness will evaluate the degree to which WHCLIS achieved the goals it set out to achieve (beyond the simple mounting of a conference). Third, the section on relevancy will attempt to resolve questions concerning the goals themselves. Was WHCLIS trying to answer the right questions? Was it the most appropriate means for achieving the most important goals?

After evaluating the White House Conference from these three perspectives, the chapter will consider the degree to which the conference was, at a cost of $3.5 million, the most effective use of resources for the promotion of library and information services. WHCLIS will be compared with other White House conferences, with alternative expenditures of library funding, and with other approaches to achieving identified goals. Finally, the chapter will consider whether current conditions warrant another WHCLIS.

HISTORY AND ORGANIZATION

The White House Conference on Library and Information Services was held on November 15-19, 1979. As an event, WHCLIS was unprecedented. It was both the first White House conference to deal with library and information services, and the largest White House conference ever held at one location.

The idea of a conference was introduced more than 20 years earlier by Channing Bete, a library trustee from Greenfield, MA, at a 1957 meeting of the American Library Trustee Association. Although the idea was one whose time had not yet come, the dream of a White House conference survived, with support from the American Library Association, for four presidential administrations. In 1974 Congress finally passed a bill (PL 93-568) authorizing and requesting the president to call a White House Conference on Library and Information Services. In January 1977 President Ford named 15 persons to the official White House Conference Advisory Committee. Later that year, President Carter signed the FY 1977 Supplemental Appropriations Bill that allocated $3.5 million for WHCLIS.

Purpose and Principles

According to PL 93-568, WHCLIS was intended "to develop recommendations for the further improvement of the nation's libraries and information centers and their use by the public." The legislation further specified that WHCLIS should set goals consistent with seven conditions and principles:

• Access to information and ideas is indispensable to the development of human potential, the advancement of civilization and the continuance of enlightened self-government.

• The preservation and the dissemination of information and ideas are the primary purpose and function of libraries and information centers.

• The growth and augmentation of the nation's libraries and information centers are essential if all Americans are to have reasonable access to adequate services of libraries and information centers.

• New achievements in technology offer a potential for enabling libraries and information centers to serve the public more fully, expeditiously and economically.

• Maximum realization of the potential inherent in the use of advanced technology by libraries and information centers requires cooperation through planning for, and coordination of, the services of libraries and information centers.

• The National Commission on Libraries and Information Science is developing plans for meeting national needs for library and information services, and for coordinating activities to meet those needs.

• Productive recommendations for expanding access to libraries and information centers will require public understanding and support as well as that of public and private libraries and information centers.

Selection of Staff and Delegates

As is the case with many worthwhile undertakings, the course of the White House

Conference did not run smoothly. In May 1978 Dr. Frederick Burkhardt, chairman of the National Commission on Libraries and Information Science (NCLIS) and WHCLIS, retired. Subsequently, Charles Benton was appointed as his replacement, Marilyn Killebrew Gell (now Marilyn Mason) was named director of WHCLIS, and President Carter named a new White House Conference Advisory Committee.

Unlike many conferences, WHCLIS was more than a single event. It was preceded by two years of planning and preparation, much of which took place at 58 state and regional conferences. These meetings provided an opportunity for broad participation in defining the issues that the conference would address, while also serving as the primary vehicle for delegate selection.

PL 93-568 required only that WHCLIS bring together:

• Representatives of local, statewide, regional and national institutions, agencies, organizations, and associations that provide library and information services to the public;

• Representatives of educational institutions, agencies, organizations, and associations (including professional and scholarly associations for the advancement of education and research);

• Persons with special knowledge of, and special competence in, technology as it may be used for the improvement of library and information services; and

• Representatives of federal, state and local governments, professional and lay people, and other members of the general public.

However, it was clear from Congressional testimony that Congress intended WHCLIS to be more than a gathering of library professionals. Early in the planning process, guidelines were promulgated that required the ratio of delegates to be one-third library and information services professionals and two-thirds lay persons or community representatives. In addition, the planning group decided that the delegates should be as fully representative of the general public as was reasonable. To this end, 568 delegates were selected at state and regional conferences, to ensure a geographic distribution and democratic approach. There were also 105 delegates-at-large appointed by the Advisory Committee, to correct any inequities that may have resulted from the pre-conference selection process and to ensure further full representation by all parts of society.

In addition to the 58 state and territorial conferences held prior to November 1979, five "theme" conferences were also convened, as a means of generating discussion about specific topics that were of special concern at the time. These topics were: federal funding alternatives, the structure and governance of library networks, libraries and literacy, international information exchange, and new communication and information technology.

Resolutions poured in to the WHCLIS staff from both the theme conferences and the state and territorial conferences. Altogether, there were over 3000 resolutions generated by over 100,000 people. The WHCLIS staff reviewed the resolutions, grouped them by user needs, and commissioned individual authors who were knowledgeable in each specific area to prepare discussion guides to assist delegates at the conference.

MAJOR ISSUES AND CONFERENCE THEMES

The major issues selected for discussion indicate the range and variety of topics that delegates later addressed. Some of those issues are summarized here, listed under category headings that later became conference themes.

Meeting Personal Needs

• What new services should library and information providers offer to meet personal needs?

• What national policy issues must be addressed if libraries and information services are to be more effective in meeting personal needs?

• How should library and information services be expanded or redesigned to meet the needs of special constituencies?

• What legislative and funding initiatives are required to encourage better use of limited resources in our nation's libraries?

• What measures will encourage maximum use of the nation's information resources?

Enhancing Lifelong Learning

• How could the present federal legislative program supporting library and information services (school, public and academic) be more effectively administered?

• What are the respective roles and areas for increased cooperation between school and public libraries in meeting the needs of school-aged children?

• How best can a nationwide network be implemented to support the nation's educational goals?

• How can libraries and information services improve and enhance the lifelong learning opportunities of the nation's citizens?

• How can libraries and information services best be used to promote literacy?

• What increases should there be in the percentage of state support of the total funding of public libraries and what are the dimensions of the federal role?

• What special status, if any, should be accorded by the federal government for those academic and research libraries with collections of regional and national significance?

• How can local community, public school and academic libraries and information services that support our national educational programs adapt to the changing social and technological environment?

Improving Organizations and the Professions

• What new roles and services should libraries and other information providers assume in serving organizations and professions?

• What kinds of information delivery services should be used to meet the needs of organizations and professions?

• How can libraries and information providers best serve the needs of special constituencies such as professional groups and non-profit organizations?

• What should be the roles of the federal government and the private sector in providing information services and systems that serve organizations and professions?

• To what extent should information be made available to individual and organizational users?

Effectively Governing Society

• How best can we distribute information needed for governing society?

• Should government share its legislative information system developed by the Congressional Research Service?

• What new government information services can libraries offer?

• What is the appropriate balance between freedom of information and individual privacy?

• How do we ensure the preservation of information sources necessary for governing society?

• Do we need a national information policy?

Increasing International Cooperation

• In a pluralistic world, do Americans need more information from abroad? Do other peoples need new types of information from the United States? If so, how can these needs be met?

• How can comprehensive and well-articulated policies and procedures for sharing United States' information best be developed?

• As technology advances, how can the goal of broader information flow be balanced with the rights of private corporations and nation-states to control the information they generate?

• How should the underlying international imbalance in the ability to create and disseminate information be reduced?

• How can the United States help the developing countries meet their information and communication needs?

CONFERENCE RESOLUTIONS AND RECOMMENDATIONS

These issues, and many more, were discussed and debated by the 806 official delegates and alternates to WHCLIS in the days and nights between November 15 and November 19. The four and one-half days of the Conference itself, with its speeches, hearings, work sessions and social sessions, have been described fully in *Information for the 1980s: The Final Report of the White House Conference.* (See Bibliography.)

The resolutions passed at WHCLIS were almost as wide-ranging as the issues from which they flowed. Delegates approved 64 in all—25 by voice vote and 39 by paper ballot. The resolutions called for some major changes in some aspects of library and information services, and reaffirmed some long-held beliefs and commitments in other areas.

The three goals that seem to permeate all of the resolutions proved to be an accurate indicator of the political mood of the country. They were: to reshape library and information services to serve the people in more useful ways, to maintain local control of these services, and to insist on more economy and accountability from the institutions that provide the services.

The WHCLIS report summarizes some of the specific recommendations included in the resolutions:

> Resolutions urge libraries to take an increased role in literacy training; in im-
> proving access to information for all, including ethnic minority groups, blind
> persons, physically handicapped persons, and others who are not adequately
> served. They favor increased activity by the United States to encourage the
> free flow of information among nations. Many endorse the idea of the
> library as both a total community information center and as an independent
> learning center. Generally, the resolutions support the concept of the library
> as essential to a civilized society, a concern the government must view with
> high priority in the decision-making process. Delegates to the Conference also
> emphasized the importance of technology and considered ways this nation
> can use it to improve library and information services. They discussed and
> refined such concepts as the linking of public telecommunications and the
> Postal Service with a new, expanded role for libraries.

Based on the resolutions, elements of a national library and information services program were compiled, and an outline for a proposed National Library and Information Ser-

vices Act was drawn up. With high hopes, the final report was presented to President Carter on March 21, 1980. Afterward, the President assembled an Interagency Task Force to study the resolutions and recommend action.

PRESIDENT'S MESSAGE TO CONGRESS

In late September 1980, the President addressed many of the WHCLIS recommendations in a message to Congress. In the message, President Carter reaffirmed the importance of libraries and recommended the following federal initiatives (listed here under categorical headings).

The Importance of Libraries

In confirming the importance of libraries and information services, the President recommended the following:

• The submission of new legislation to replace the Library Services and Construction Act (LSCA); and

• Increased budgetary support for resource sharing among and innovative application of technologies to libraries and research libraries.

Government Information

To improve access to and management of government information, President Carter suggested that the federal government:

• Use the Office of Management and Budget to help develop federal information policy;

• Affirm the key role of the federal depository libraries where citizens can obtain free access to government information; and

• Direct, for the first time, that Federal Information Centers be located in libraries (initially three to five, but to be expanded if successful).

Needs of the Disadvantaged

To address the needs of the handicapped and disadvantaged, the President indicated that he would:

• Direct the Department of Education to take the lead in coordinating federal efforts to eliminate functional illiteracy, which affects 20% of all Americans;

• Direct the Department of the Interior to analyze and recommend steps for reducing the impact of barriers to information access for the geographically remote; and

• Send to the Senate a protocol to the Florence Agreement further liberalizing the exchange of books and information and reducing barriers to international understanding.

New Information and Communication Technologies

Acknowledging the increasing importance of the new technologies, President Carter indicated that his administration would:

• Continue working with the Federal Communications Commission in the overhaul of its regulations, opening competition and promoting diversity;

• Continue to work on developing standards that will enhance our ability to transfer technology;

• Continue to work on removing regulations that prevent competition and constrain application of the new technologies;

• Work with the Congress to pass legislation to reduce regulations, stimulate innovation, increase productivity and make communications industries more responsive to consumer demands;

• Direct the Commerce Department to work with the library community to make satellites and other technologies available, where cost-effective, for networking; and

• Encourage the library and information science communities to propose technology assessment studies for consideration by federal agencies.

In the message, the President also affirmed the role of libraries as community resources for information for the consumer and small business on such matters as energy, marketing and technological innovations.

THE VIEW OF THE REAGAN ADMINISTRATION

Four months after President Carter delivered his message to Congress, Ronald Reagan replaced him as president. Announcing his intention to "get the government off our backs," President Reagan began to dismantle many of the social-service activities of the federal government. Under the Reagan administration, the National Library and Information Services Act has, for all intents and purposes, been abandoned. Funding cuts at the federal level have also halted new initiatives and severely impaired the ability of library-related agencies to provide support. A dangerously declining economy has further eroded the financial base of most libraries, sending many scrambling for the funding necessary to maintain their most basic services.

Finally, as discussed in Chapter 6, the federal government appears to be on the brink of abrogating its responsibility for information distribution. The Freedom of Information Act is under attack. Federal information distribution centers such as NTIS have lost support, and the Justice Department's suit against AT&T has been resolved in favor of the world's largest corporation. Even NCLIS, the agency responsible for the White House Conference and thought to be sensitive to the public need for information, has issued a report that recommends the shifting of responsibility away from the public sector to private industry.

In the face of these developments, an evaluation of the efficiency, effectiveness and relevancy of the White House Conference takes on special significance.

EFFICIENCY

There is no perfect way to run a conference, even a White House conference. There were, however, several decisions made quite early in the planning process that contributed materially to the success of WHCLIS. As a result of those decisions, the national conference was preceded by state and territorial conferences; the structure of the national conference was designed to encourage the highest degree of participation possible by delegates; and the delegates were broadly representative of the general population, with the majority chosen from among those served by libraries rather than librarians themselves. Because these decisions contributed more to the effectiveness of the conference than its efficiency, they will be considered in more detail in that section. They are mentioned here, however, because they helped determine the design of the conference.

The major thrust of these policy decisions was to create as democratic a process as possible, a design that flowed from a belief that the exchange of information and opinion is vital to the development of libraries as well as other public institutions. While the merit of a democratic process may seem obvious to many, it is not always found in White House conferences, and there were some special interest groups that did not feel it was appropriate to WHCLIS.

Comparison with Earlier White House Conferences

Historically, White House conferences have served one of two purposes. They have been used as either a vehicle for promoting legislation that the current administration wanted passed, or as a means of proposing new policy initiatives. The White House Conference on Education that took place in the 1960s is a good example of the first type. That conference was called by Lyndon Johnson to promote a package of education legislation. It was generally considered a successful conference because much of the recommended legislation was passed, and because most of the legislation is still with us today. Other recent White House conferences that have followed this model include the 1980 White House Conference on Small Business and the 1981 White House Conference on the Aging.

During the planning for WHCLIS, many in the library field indicated that they would prefer a conference structure that focused delegates' attention and lobbying efforts on specific legislation. But others felt just as strongly that they did not want to be a "rubber stamp" in a "managed conference." Because there were so many strong and conflicting feelings about the purpose of the conference, there was some controversy about the selection of the theme areas described earlier in this chapter. In retrospect, it is clear that there was nothing magic or definitive about the theme areas chosen. Their purpose was to provide a mechanism whereby delegates could participate in the development of conference resolutions as fully as possible.

Evaluation

Viewed as an event, WHCLIS must be judged a qualified success, if only because 3500 delegates were accommodated for four and one-half days and nights of meetings and activities that resulted in the passage of 64 resolutions. Delegates and other participants achieved what they came to achieve. They met, they deliberated, they listened to speeches, they attended social events, and they reached conclusions.

In a post-conference evaluation, delegates were asked to respond to questions concerning all aspects of the conference. The vast majority of those participating in the evaluation felt that WHCLIS had achieved what they hoped it would achieve. Some felt that there were too many speeches, that there was not enough time for delegates to deliberate, that there was too much or not enough time for social events, and that time should have been scheduled for sleeping. In general, however, delegates were pleased with their work and felt that the results reflected their best efforts.

EFFECTIVENESS

No matter how successful WHCLIS may have been as an event, it would be meaningless if it did not achieve what it set out to achieve. Thus, an evaluation of the conference's effectiveness in achieving its long-term goals is critical.

According to the legislation, the purpose of WHCLIS was "to develop recommendations for the further improvement of the nation's libraries and information centers and their use by the public." In addition, the conference had an implied purpose: to develop an environment in which the recommendations could be realized.

As noted above, early decisions concerning the selection of delegates, the holding of state and territorial conferences, and the structure of the national conference determined that the White House Conference would be truly democratic in nature. Debate and discussion were expected among a wide variety of people, at both the White House Conference itself and at the local conferences that preceded it. This process involved over 100,000 people nationwide, and it contributed both to the formulation of recommendations and to the establishment of a hospitable environment.

State and Local Initiatives

Had the conference focused exclusively on federal actions, it would have to be viewed as more a failure than a success. In 1980 the election of Ronald Reagan stopped the momentum toward increased federal responsibility in library development. While library programs have not yet actually been cut (thanks in many ways to the dedicated effort of

WHCLIS delegates), the more exciting federal initiatives that were proposed have at least been temporarily abandoned.

Fortunately, delegates have recognized the need to continue action at the local level, and to form regionally and locally based special interest groups to work for change at the federal level. The same democratic principles that informed the conference have guided the actions of these state and local "friends groups" as they have lobbied for new legislation passed at the state level. Moreover, many of these efforts have been coordinated and shared through the White House Conference on Library and Information Services Task Force (WHCLIST), a group of delegate representatives responsible for the implementation of WHCLIS recommendations.

Summary of State Activity

A 1982 report compiled by Laura Chodos, a member of the WHCLIST Steering Committee, revealed that the following state activity has taken place in the period since the 1979 White House Conference:

• Legislation Authorizing Budget Increases. Nineteen states passed budgetary increases for public or for state library agencies in 1982; 20 states and one territory passed such legislation in 1981.

• Legislation Authorizing Funds for Library Automation or Resource Sharing. In 1982, 10 states passed legislation authorizing state aid for library automation or equipment necessary for interlibrary cooperation. In 1981, six states and three territories passed similar legislation.

• General Legislation. In 1982, 21 states passed a wide range of legislation concerning libraries. The legislation addressed areas such as school/public library cooperation, support for library construction, computer literacy programs and confidentiality of library records.

• Public Awareness Programs. Twenty-one states embarked on specific activities to heighten library visibility in 1982, while 24 states and four territories reported such activities in 1981. WHCLIST has also spearheaded the development of a national library logo that has been adopted by the American Library Association and that is being used by libraries across the country.

• Statewide Friends Groups/Citizen Library Councils. Eight states reported the formation of new friends groups in 1982, in addition to the 24 states and two territories reporting new groups in 1981. Some states with existing friends groups have seen membership grow significantly.

• Extension of Library Services. Thirteen states reported new or expanded statewide efforts to serve nontraditional or handicapped users in 1982; 17 states and one territory initiated new services in 1981.

• Expansion of Library Services. Fourteen states in 1982 and six states and one territory in 1981 reported the expansion of services corresponding to specific White House Conference resolutions.

• Continuing Library Education. Six states in 1982 and 12 states in 1981 reported special efforts to develop needed workshops and seminars.

• New Publications. Twenty-seven states reported newly published studies, reports, needs assessments and other publications such as long-range plans in 1982, while 14 states and one territory reported similar activity in 1981.

• State-Level Changes in Library Responsibility. Seven states experienced changes in state-level authority over library matters or changes in the state-level activity, including new library authorities and the collaboration of archives and library agencies.[1]

WHCLIST does not claim that all of the above actions are directly attributable to the White House Conference. Members of WHCLIST do feel, however, that the contribution of White House Conference delegates and other participants has been a significant factor in accomplishing change throughout the states.

Continuing Efforts

Many have called the resolutions passed at WHCLIS a "laundry list." Indeed, from one perspective, the resolutions seem to include a little something for everyone. On the other hand, since the resolutions were the result of a democratic process, each delegate owns a piece of the list, and most have been willing to help work toward the goals contained in the resolutions. Currently, while the federal government remains unresponsive, WHCLIS delegates have turned their energies to building state support. They have not, however, abandoned hope that federal initiatives may be possible in the future.

WHCLIS was successful in achieving its articulated purpose of developing recommendations, and the conference has been at least partially successful in achieving its implied purpose of creating an environment in which those recommendations can be enacted. However, there is clearly much more to be achieved. In a political environment, there is never any final resolution, since priorities and circumstances continually shift and change. But libraries are making progress, slowly and deliberately to be sure, but making progress nevertheless. Moreover, at least some of the progress is a result of WHCLIS and the thousands of concerned citizens who participated in it and continue to promote its recommendations and resolutions.

RELEVANCY

Relevancy issues are generally the hardest to address because they question the conference goals themselves. Nevertheless, in order to assess the full impact of WHCLIS, it is important to look closely at what the conference was designed to accomplish. An evaluation of efficiency and effectiveness asks: "Did we do things right?" An evaluation of relevancy asks: "Did we do the right things?"

The section on effectiveness looked at the degree to which the conference achieved its mission. This section will ask if there could have been a better way to achieve that mission. Could the human and financial investment made in WHCLIS have been better spent in direct provision of library services, in research and development, or in some other activity?

Expenditures

While the federal investment in WHCLIS was relatively modest (about $3.5 million), the purpose was relatively ambitious: to develop recommendations for the further improvement of the nation's libraries and information centers and their use by the public. Criticisms of expenditures for WHCLIS usually fall into one of three general areas: 1) the amount available was far too small to do the job; 2) the money could have been better spent in some other library-related activity; and 3) the development of recommendations was a waste of time and money anyway.

To put the expenditure in perspective, it is useful to look at the conference budget in several contexts. On the one hand, total public library expenditures for 1977 were $1.5 billion, or about 500 times the cost of the White House Conference. On the other hand, HEA Title II-B funding specifically allocated for library research totaled only $1 million in 1976. The White House Conference expenditure was three and one-half times that. While it is hard to guess what the long-term impact of $3.5 million spent on research would be, the impact of the investment in the conference can be measured. Descriptions of accomplishments within states are outlined above.

Key Questions

But questions remain. Was the amount allocated sufficient to accomplish the purpose of the conference? Could the money have been better spent? Do the recommendations really matter?

The answer in each case is, "It depends." Certainly, $3.5 million was not sufficient to accomplish the task completely or perfectly. It was, however, sufficient to make progress. As far as there being better uses for the money, that depends on what one sees as the most significant objective to be achieved in the library field. From the perspectives of delegates favoring particular programs or representing specific interests, the money might have been better spent if the conference's purposes, both articulated and implied, were altered. Finally, the recommendations "matter" only if one believes that public participation in policy development is important. There is no ideal set of recommendations, just as there is no fully satisfactory solution to most of the problems that afflict our institutions and organizations.

Ultimately, the entire discussion hinges on one's perception of politics and problem solving. As noted in Chapter 6, centralized federal planning has not been particularly effective. Thus, recommendations for federal action cannot be seen as an end in themselves. It is important to keep the implied goal of the conference—to create a receptive environment—in mind. In many ways, the White House Conference served to decentralize and democratize planning and policy making. In a final analysis, that may be its greatest success. WHCLIS gave a great many people a stake in the future of library and information services.

CONCLUSION

If there is one overwhelming lesson to be learned from the White House Conference, it is that democracy works. It works in the short-term context of an event, and it works in the longer-range context of policy development. That is not to say that it works efficiently, or that it is completely satisfying for all participants. Like most exercises in consensus building, there is a great deal of compromise as participants learn more about other points of view.

If one looks only at the number of recommendations that have been implemented since 1979, WHCLIS was disappointing. On the federal level in particular, progress has been slight. On the state and local level, however, progress has been substantial. Moreover, the energy, enthusiasm and efforts of WHCLIS participants continue to a degree that was probably not envisioned by Channing Bete in 1957.

More than anything else, the White House Conference gave people who care about libraries a voice. WHCLIS provided them with a mechanism for working together productively. It helped them organize an effective special interest group that can and has been used to plan and lobby for more responsive library and information services. As long as our form of government continues to deliver the level of services the majority of people want and are willing to pay taxes for, planning and consensus building will remain important activities.

Many White House conferences are held every 10 years. Some of those, such as the White House Conference on Aging, have enabled special constituencies to make real progress in improving public policies that affect them. Issues in the library and information service area are on the ascendency. Driven by technological change, the capacities of our institutions to respond to the information needs of the public are changing daily. This suggests that, in the near future at least, one other White House Conference on Library and Information Services would be appropriate.

There are questions about library and information services that will never be completely answered, and issues that will never be completely resolved. Sometimes, when dealing with important public policy, it is more important that the questions be asked than that answers be found.

FOOTNOTES

1. Laura B. Chodos, Lucille Thomas and Gladys Ann Wells, compilers, *Third Annual Report From the States: 1982 White House Conference on Library and Information Services Follow-up Inquiry.* Unpublished document presented at follow-up meeting of White House Conference on Library and Information Services Task Force (WHCLIST), Atlanta, GA, September 24-26, 1982.

9

The Future Federal Role

This book has examined the history of federal involvement in library and information services; the political, economic and technological trends that shape the environment in which federal policies are developed; and current federal activity in specific library and information service areas. As individual chapters have demonstrated, the federal role has grown significantly since the founding of our nation. This growth has been consistent with the changing responsibilities of government and the evolving needs of individuals and society.

Although some of the conclusions presented in previous chapters are interpretive, they are based on an analysis of identifiable data. Predicting the future is a trickier business. Arthur Clarke, a reasonably successful predictor of future events, has identified the two most common hazards confronting the would-be prophet: failure of nerve and failure of imagination. Failure of nerve occurs when an individual, given all the relevant facts, cannot see that they lead to an inescapable conclusion. Failure of imagination arises when an individual analyzes available data accurately, but fails to anticipate the impact of undiscovered information and future events. Thus the failure to imagine the impact of X-rays, nuclear energy, radio and television, and transistors before their discovery or invention would have been a failure of imagination; while the failure to recognize the potential impact of the automobile, television or microcomputers after their development would be a failure of nerve.

In analyzing the future of the federal role in library and information services, this chapter does not pretend to anticipate what would happen in the event of a nuclear disaster, severe economic disruption or major technological breakthrough. Instead, the predictions it offers are based on the assumption that the future will flow from past and present federal policies, and that policy developments will be shaped by evolving political, economic and technological conditions. In other words, the chapter views the continuing development of federal library and information policy as more of an evolutionary than revolutionary process. However, it will try to avoid a "failure of nerve" resulting from a failure to assess potential and probable changes.

The following sections describe the latest political, economic and technological trends that are likely to affect the future activity of the federal government. They analyze the impact of these forces on the four federal roles discussed throughout this book: data collection and distribution, financial support through grants-in-aid, research and demonstration, and planning and policy making. Finally, the chapter identifies reasonable objectives for federal participation in the development of library and information services, and suggests ways in which individuals might help shape and promote those goals and objectives.

POLITICAL, ECONOMIC AND TECHNOLOGICAL TRENDS

Chapter 2 described how tension and ambiguity have characterized the balance of power in the American democracy, and how three major values embedded in that balance have shaped the nation's development: individual rights, states' rights and property rights. It also pointed out that these values are most often experienced as conflicts between competing values: 1) freedom of the individual versus the good of the people as a whole; 2) sovereignty of the states versus the sovereignty of the federal government; and 3) private sector economic interests versus public sector responsibilities.

The Changing Balance

Additional examination suggests that there is a tension not only between values within each of the three categories but among the categories as well. As a nation, we appear to have moved from an initial concern about individual rights through a period of preoccupation with states rights. Currently, we seem infatuated with property rights.

This philosophical shift can be seen in every area of federal policy making. For the first time in our history, the federal government is turning away from its responsibility to provide information needed for the operation of the government itself. Attacks on grants-in-aid programs continue, and research in non-military areas has been curtailed. In addition, recent developments in federal information policy appear to constitute an assault on the public's "right to know." In each of these areas, government actions have been justified on the basis of the need to protect and support private enterprise.

Economic and Technological Trends

In mid-1983, the nation appears to be recovering from one of the most severe recessions in recent memory. Inflation has slowed, interest rates have stabilized and most economic indicators point to a gradual recovery. Nevertheless, unemployment remains high, and funding for social and economic programs continues to be threatened.

Debate over the economic responsibility of the federal government to provide funding for public education was renewed in early 1983 with the publication of the report of the National Commission on Excellence in Education (NCEE). In the report, NCEE concluded that our nation is at risk because the quality of public education is so poor. Released a few months before the first round of presidential primaries, the NCEE report has made education a major issue for the 1984 election. In doing so, the NCEE conclusions have touched off new discussions about the appropriate roles for federal, state and local governments in supporting education.

Just what this means for library and information services is difficult to say. At the federal level, library funding has always been closely tied to educational support, and the presence of the library programs in the Department of Education further strengthens that relationship. In the spring of 1983, the Department of Education requested proposals for a study titled "Alternative Funding Possibilities for Publicly Supported Library and Information Services." The request set off a fire-storm of protest within the library field, since it seems to be based on the assumption that libraries are expendable and that private support is a realistic alternative.

As Chapter 2 pointed out, the economic justification for public support of libraries rests on the theory of public goods. However, the current and continuing debates over support for libraries and information services make it quite clear that the real issues go well beyond economic arguments and rest ultimately on considerations of social value and political reality.

The current reality that may ultimately have the greatest impact on the federal role in library development is the increasing importance of computer and communications technologies. Many see these new technologies as the hope of the future. Others fear the power that these devices can place in the hands of the few and the potential for abusing that power. Whatever one's positions on these issues, it is clear that information technologies will change the way libraries do business, and that the technologies may bring about major changes in the federal government's own information collection and distribution activities.

DATA COLLECTION AND DISTRIBUTION

Since the Continental Congress met in Philadelphia in 1774 and arranged with the Library Company of Philadelphia to furnish materials to delegates, the United States has recognized the need to provide the information our nation's leaders require to make legislative decisions. The Library of Congress itself was established early in this nation's history. By 1983 the federal government was supporting three national libraries and a broad network of federal libraries charged with the responsibility of providing information needed to run our government.

As Chapter 3 pointed out, the federal government is also a producer and distributor of information. While the government is most likely to continue to provide for its own information needs, expectations concerning its role in distributing information to the public vary. Dissemination of government information has already dropped off sharply as a result of policy changes described in Chapter 6.

In the area of data collection, federal activities are likely to be a continuation of past and current operations. Moreover, the national libraries can be expected to continue their leadership role in developing new library services and testing new technologies. As before, services and methods developed at the federal level will be picked up and used by other libraries across the country.

However, the current move to have some federal library services performed by private contractors could threaten the federal libraries' leadership role. In the near future, it is probable that the government will close some small federal libraries. Privately, a few federal librarians even admit that a number of smaller libraries in the system, particularly those that are less effective and efficient, should be eliminated. If this happens, some of the services that were offered by the discontinued libraries may be picked up by private concerns, probably through various kinds of computerized delivery systems. In contrast, over the next decade, the national libraries and the majority of larger federal libraries will probably continue their current levels of operation. In fact, some observers feel that the current period of stagnation may be followed by a period of considerable expansion.

Federal information distribution activities are on shakier ground. As of mid-1983, 2000 government publications had already been eliminated, and budget reductions had been proposed for an additional 2300 publications. Funding reductions are also proposed for the depository library program for FY 1984, and the National Technical Information Service remains under attack. These actions flow from the political philosophies outlined above and, since they represent major changes in policy, they will be discussed at greater length below, in the section on planning and policy making.

GRANTS-IN-AID PROGRAMS

In spite of repeated threats and administrative requests for zero-funding, library grants-in-aid programs have maintained their modest funding levels during the Reagan administration. Surprisingly, President Reagan even approved an appropriation for Title II of the Library Services and Construction Act, the first funding LSCA Title II has received in 10 years.

Going into 1984, the outlook for library grants-in-aid programs is more positive than one might expect. The reasons for this are political rather than philosophical (although there are also a number of economic and technological reasons that will be discussed later in the chapter). First, despite the Reagan administration's efforts, grants-in-aid programs have held their own during the difficult first three years of the 1980s. Second, libraries now have effective lobbying groups, both in Washington and throughout the nation. On the state and national levels, the follow-up group from the 1979 White House Conference continues to operate and can be counted on to mount an effective campaign when the time is right.

Finally, libraries may be able to piggyback their funding and lobbying efforts on the call for improvements in education. This was the strategy in 1956 when the Library Services Act was first introduced, and it was the strategy in the 1960s when library funding was substantially increased in the wake of major education legislation. Education has already become a major issue in the 1984 presidential campaign, and increased federal support is likely.

For federal grants-in-aid programs, political action by the library community will be the key to success. Fortunately, library supporters have become relatively sophisticated practitioners of political strategy in recent years, and political balances appear to be beginning a shift toward a more positive direction.

RESEARCH AND DEVELOPMENT

Although arguments for federal support of research and development are intellectually compelling, they have never been particularly successful in generating funding. Unfortunately, this trend is likely to continue. In coming years, research in defense-related programs will probably increase, as will research into issues related to technology and industrial productivity. Compared to groups with a vested interest in these areas, the political constituency concerned about library and information service research is small and not particularly vocal. As suggested earlier, library lobbyists have tended to emphasize the need for grants-in-aid programs over the less immediate research and development needs.

In spite of this pessimistic outlook, there are several avenues that, if pursued, might provide increased federal support for library R&D. The first of these is for libraries to find ways to tap into federal funds targeted for technology and productivity-related research. This can be accomplished by making sure that library and information-related services are included among the areas eligible for funding. The second strategy is to push HEA Title II-B as part of the grants-in-aid package. This has not been successful in the past, but it might be worth another attempt. The third option is to develop either a legislative or regulatory mechanism that would permit (even require) recipients of federal funds to allocate some portion of those monies to research and development. Of course, the details of such an approach would need to be worked out by those affected.

PLANNING AND POLICY MAKING

As suggested above, and as described in detail in Chapter 6, information policy is closely tied to political philosophy. Currently, most of the pressing issues in information policy appear to be generated by the philosophical conflict between individual rights and property rights. More specifically, the relationship between public and private information services and interests is becoming increasingly confused, and it is likely to become even more confusing as both sectors grow larger and more powerful.

This confusion is likely to continue for a long time. The next 10 to 20 years will probably be characterized by tension and struggle to achieve balance between public and private sector interests. Even now, the issues are poorly defined and far from resolution.

Federal policies toward the distribution of government information are one example of the type of problem found in this area. Under the Reagan administration, the Paperwork Reduction Act has been used to reduce the flow of information to the public. Some say this results in economy in government, and some find the reduction appropriate because it lessens government competition with private information firms. But others contend that the government is simply abandoning its responsibility to inform its citizens. The future does not appear to hold any quick or easy solutions.

In the future, most federal publications that have already been eliminated will probably not be resurrected, regardless of the particular administration or political party in power. For the near term, at least, there is likely to be a greater role for private organizations in the distribution of federally generated information. Although the fate of the National Technical Information Service (NTIS) is difficult to predict, given natural bureaucratic inertia, NTIS will more likely be weakened than eliminated altogether.

The move toward deregulation is also likely to continue, vesting an increasing amount of power in the hands of those private companies that control our lines of communication and information. Meanwhile, electronic surveillance capabilities will grow more sophisticated, making privacy an increasingly important policy concern. Other information policy issues detailed in Chapter 6 will also take on more importance as the new information technologies begin to touch the lives of every American.

In the area of library planning, there is likely to be a continuation of the trend toward decentralization. In fact, the two most successful major developments in recent library history have both been the result of decentralized planning. The first was the growth and development of state library agencies through Library Services and Construction Act (LSCA) regulations requiring that each state prepare a library plan. The second has been the decentralized development of networking. These developments are described in Chapters 4 and 7.

FUTURE FEDERAL OBJECTIVES

The information presented in the preceding chapters and the general predictions outlined above suggest some reasonable objectives for future federal involvement in library and information services. The objectives listed below are based on both past and present experience, as well as on key political, economic and technological considerations. Several of the objectives are drawn from earlier chapters, where they were included in discussions of library networking and federal information policies.

• *Support national libraries and federal libraries as important national resources.* It is imperative that decision makers within the federal government have access to information. The contribution that national and federal libraries make to this goal is significant and well documented. Moreover, in many instances federal libraries play an important role in library development nationwide, thereby increasing general public access to information.

• *Encourage the expansion of state and local resources by providing financial incentives for library development.* This objective would result in an extension of current grants-in-aid programs. It is based on the assumption that support for libraries should be a responsibility that is shared by several levels of government. While many may argue the relative responsibilities of local, state and federal governments, it is clear that the federal government has a responsibility to encourage worthwhile social programs. Usually, it does this by providing financial incentives. Since this approach has been especially effective in library programs, it should be continued.

• *Encourage the continued growth of major research libraries by subsidizing resource development.* Major research libraries are an important national resource. Most research libraries serve individuals far beyond their geographic boundaries, and they provide the means for the advancement of knowledge on a national scale. Unfortunately, as expenses have increased, the number of research libraries has diminished. As technological advancement makes it easier for the remaining libraries to share their resources, it will become even more important that they be given direct subsidy by the federal government, both to maintain their collections and to make their materials available to a growing user population.

• *Support research and development at an elevated level to achieve economies of scale, increased productivity and advances in information technology that might have a spillover effect on other parts of the economy.* Potentially, developments in information technology can provide the means for libraries to increase their productivity and expand their public services. Unfortunately, research and demonstration projects focusing on new technologies are too expensive for most individual libraries to undertake. By supporting regional and cooperative projects, the federal government could help bring the benefits of information research to all libraries. In addition, research in information areas has unarguable spillover effects that would appear to justify large-scale federal support.

• *Promote the use of the latest technology within the government itself, so that federal agencies become a model for information handling and spin-off systems.* The Library of Congress has already shown the value of this approach, and this objective is already embodied, to some extent, in the Paperwork Reduction Act. It is unclear in 1983, however, to what extent this goal is being pursued.

• *Limit centralized planning and policy making.* The last 10 years have been characterized by an infatuation with the notion that library planning should be centralized. As described earlier, experience in a number of areas suggests that planning is most effective when it involves those who will be affected by it. It is least effective when it is conducted at the federal level and then "sold" to those who must make it work. Of course, communication and coordination are valuable and should be promoted. Centralized planning, however, is in conflict both with our national political bias toward local control and the trend toward distributed and decentralized systems in information technology.

• *Provide a mechanism for the establishment and promulgation of technical standards.* In apparent conflict with the preceding objective, this objective is based on the perceived need for generally accepted technical standards. In this instance, some centralization is important. It is also consistent with library experience over the last century.

• *Adopt a laissez-faire approach to the development of bibliographic utilities and state and regional networks, with the exception of support for R&D.* Although this objective conflicts with current rhetoric, it represents a continuation of current practice. Philosophically, it flows from the non-interventionist posture described above.

• *Maintain a balanced approach to federal information distribution.* As described in Chapter 6, federal information distribution is a complex issue that touches on privacy, freedom of information, individual rights and property rights. As a result, balance is difficult to achieve. In 1983 the scale appears to be tilted away from public access to government information and an individual's right to know. Returning a balance to federal policies toward information distribution is probably the most difficult and important of the federal library and information-related objectives listed here.

The objectives listed above are deliberately limited. They do not suggest that the federal government should try to be all things to all people. In that sense, they are consistent with political trends, economic imperatives and technological capabilities. They do, however, recognize that the federal government has an important responsibility to provide the means for its citizens to acquire information and knowledge.

CONCLUSION

The federal government is in the information business, whether it wants to be or not. It maintains libraries and information services necessary for its own operation; it provides funding through grants-in-aid programs; it engages in research and development; and it makes policy. These activities are necessary and appropriate.

In conducting the business of government, elected officials make choices. Sometimes these choices appear to impede rather than promote the distribution of information. As citizens in a democracy, we have both the right and the responsibility to let our elected officials know what choices we wish them to make. Of course, political philosophy, economic condiderations and technological developments may provide important justification for the choices we recommend. In the final analysis, however, political decisions are made with an eye toward the next election. At that point, citizens exercise their ultimate power.

Fortunately, library advocates have grown more skilled in recent years. Their numbers have grown, and they have become increasingly aware of the political process. In theory, libraries are the ultimate democratic institution—the foundation for an informed electorate. Their continued effectiveness will support the continued effectiveness of our form of government. The extent to which the federal government will continue to play a role in supporting library and information services appears to rest on the degree to which library advocates understand the political process, and on their skill and will in using that process to make their voices heard.

Appendix
American Library Association Chronology of Federal Information Policy Activities, 1981-83*

• April 1981. President Reagan imposed a moratorium on the production and procurement of new audiovisual aids and government publications using the rationale that the federal government is spending too much money on public relations, publicity and advertising. "Much of this waste consists of unnecessary and expensive films, magazines, and pamphlets." (*Weekly Compilation of Presidential Documents,* April 27, 1981.) The Office of Management and Budget (OMB) issued Bulletin No. 81-16, which provided procedures and guidelines for the moratorium. All agencies were required to review and reduce planned or proposed publications and to develop a management control plan to curtail future spending on periodicals, pamphlets and audiovisual materials.

• June 1981. OMB issued a model control plan to assist agencies in developing new or improved control systems to carry out the policies and guidelines in Bulletin No. 81-16, "Elimination of Wasteful Spending on Government Periodicals, Pamphlets, and Audiovisual Products."

OMB Bulletin 81-21 required each federal agency to submit its plan for reviewing its information activities by September 1, 1981. The objective was to establish a process ". . . which forces agencies to focus on and allows us (OMB) to influence decisions on how they process, maintain, and disseminate information." Bulletin No. 81-21 also required the designation of the single official in each federal agency in the executive branch who will be responsible for information resources management as required by the Paperwork Reduction Act of 1980.

• September 1981. David Stockman, Director of OMB, issued Memorandum 81-14, requiring heads of executive departments and agencies to pay special attention to the major

---

*The original American Library Association chronology was published in the *ALA Washington Newsletter* dated July 26, 1982. Additional information included in the Appendix was obtained from subsequent issues of the *ALA Washington Newsletter.*

information centers operated or sponsored by their agencies. Among the types of information centers to be evaluated are clearinghouses, information analysis centers and resource centers. Evaluation criteria included these questions: Could the private sector provide the same or similar information services? Is the information service provided on a full-cost recovery basis?

• October 1981. OMB Bulletin 81-16, Supplement No. 1, required agency review of all existing periodicals and recurring pamphlets to reevaluate their necessity and cost-effectiveness using OMB-approved control systems. Agencies must submit a new request for all series to be continued after January 15, 1982.

Public Printer Danford Sawyer, Jr. proposed to close all Government Printing Office bookstores outside of Washington, DC, plus a few Washington locations. Approximately 24 of the 27 GPO bookstores would be closed because, it is claimed, they compete with the private sector and are losing money. (Letter to Senator Mathias, Chairman of the Joint Committee on Printing, October 9, 1981.)

The Justice Department submitted to Congress the administration's proposal to limit severely the applicability of the Freedom of Information Act. (*Washington Post,* November 28, 1981.)

• November 1981. According to the *Washington Post* (November 9, 1981), over 900 government publications have been or will be eliminated and the government claims that millions of dollars will be saved as a result.

The *Washington Post* (November 20, 1981) also reported that the Commerce Department was considering replacing the National Technical Information Service with contracts to private firms. NTIS indexes and distributes at cost thousands of federally funded technical reports and research studies.

One example of a discontinued publication is the Securities and Exchange Commission *News Digest,* hardly an ephemeral public relations piece. The SEC will continue to print it for internal use, but will no longer offer subscriptions or make it available for depository library distribution. Instead, a private firm will publish it at a 50% increase in price (from $100 to $150 per year). (Security and Exchange Commission *News Digest,* November 10, 1981.)

• December 1981. Citing budget cuts, the National Archives discontinued the inter-library loan of microfilm publications from the Fort Worth Federal Archives and Records Center. About 400,000 reels of census, diplomatic, pension and other records used heavily by genealogists were lent to libraries annually. (Letter sent from the National Archives to "All Librarians," November 30, 1981.)

• January 1982. The free Government Printing Office pamphlet *Selected U.S. Government Publications* used for years to alert readers to new general interest and consumer-oriented government documents will no longer be mailed to the public because GPO says it is too expensive to mail out every month. GPO suggests that readers subscribe to the comprehensive bibliography, the *Monthly Catalog of U.S. Government Publications*, which costs $90 a year. (*Washington Post*, January 22, 1982.)

• February 1982. The President's FY 1983 budget requested zero funding for the Library Services and Construction Act; Titles II A, B and C of the Higher Education Act, which provide funds for college library resources, research and training programs, and research libraries; and the National Commission on Libraries and Information Science. Less money was proposed for the state block grants, which contain funding for school library resources, and for the U.S. Postal Service subsidy, which supports the fourth class library rate and other nonprofit mailing rates. (Office of Management and Budget, *Budget of the U.S. Government FY 1983*.)

• March 1982. A 400% increase in the cost of an annual subscription to the *Federal Register*—from $75 to $300—went into effect. (February 25 *Federal Register*, p. 8151.) In 1981, the price of a year's subscription to the *Congressional Record* increased from $75 to $208. Senator Charles Mathias stated that circulation of the CR declined almost 20% in the last three years as the price increased. (*New York Times*, June 2, 1982.)

Many publications formerly distributed free are now available only for a fee, and government agencies are urged by OMB to start charging prices high enough to recover their costs. For example, because of budget cuts, the Agriculture Department's Economic Research Service will stop free distribution of its publications and make these reports available only on a paid subscription basis. The alternative was to curtail basic research activities. (March 29 *Federal Register*, p. 13178.)

A reference collection standby, the *Dictionary of Occupational Titles*, is threatened because 87 of the 97 jobs remaining in the Labor Department's occupational analysis division are being eliminated. (*Washington Post*, March 2, 1982.)

• April 1982. The President signed Executive Order 12356, National Security Information, which substantially increases the amount of information that can be classified. (April 6 *Federal Register*, pp. 14873-14884.) Critics see the executive order as a reversal of a 30-year government policy of automatic declassification of government documents. Although the National Archives still has the authority to review classified documents, budget cuts are likely to limit the Archives' ability to carry out this function effectively. (*Chronicle of Higher Education*, April 14, 1982.)

• May 1982. The administration supports Senate amendments to the Freedom of Information Act to restrict the type and amount of government material available to the public. (*Washington Post*, May 4, 1982.)

The government's two biggest collectors of statistics, the Census Bureau and the Bureau of Labor Statistics, have cut programs because of budget reductions. The Census Bureau has dropped numerous studies, and the Bureau of Labor Statistics has asked Congress for an emergency $5.6 million appropriation "to maintain the accuracy" of such key economic indicators as the Consumer Price Index. According to a May 4 *Washington Post* article, "Many of the programs being trimmed helped the government monitor how its programs were being used. Others helped policy makers predict economic trends." The article also quoted a business leader testifying at a congressional subcommittee hearing in March: "A million dollars saved today through short-sighted reductions in the budgets for statistical programs could lead to erroneous decisions that would cost the private and public sectors billions of dollars over the long run."

The Office of Management and Budget has agreed to make available a complete list of discontinued government publications as a way ". . . to assure an orderly and equitable transfer of discontinued government publications to the private sector." (Association of American Publishers, *Capital Letter,* May 1982.)

In April the General Services Administration closed the Washington, DC Federal Information Center, leaving the 40 information centers in other parts of the country still operating. However, citing budget cuts, walk-in services have now been eliminated, leaving only the telephone numbers and people to answer them. A saving of $260,000 of the centers' $4 million annual budget is anticipated. (*Washington Post,* May 25, 1982.)

The *New York Times* (May 10, 1982) reported that GPO destroyed $11 million worth of government publications that were not selling more than 50 copies a year or earning more than $1000 in sales a year. The millions of documents were sold as wastepaper for $760,000. Although a few copies of most titles have been kept in stock, generally people looking for one of the destroyed publications will be told to find it in one of the depository libraries.

• June 1982. In keeping with its policy to refuse to offer for public sale anything that won't yield $1000 a year in sales, GPO has selected only 25 of the 69 publications which the National Bureau of Standards (NBS) wanted to offer for public sale. As a result, the rejected publications are available to the public only through the National Technical Information Service, whose prices for NBS publications are generally two to three times higher than GPO's for the same document. (Memo from NBS official, June 14, 1982.)

Continued cutbacks on free publications result in the Health and Human Services Department no longer distributing copies of *Infant Care* without charge as it has for 58 years. (*New York Times,* June 2, 1982.)

The Office of Management and Budget permits federal agencies to begin putting out new publications and films, but OMB will keep a close eye on costs and top agency officials will monitor content. According to a preliminary count, the administration has eliminated about 2000 of the 13,000 to 15,000 publications distributed before the President's April 1981 moratorium on government books, periodicals and audiovisuals. (*Washington Post,* June 11, 1982.)

• September 1982. OMB published a notice in *Federal Register* (September 8, pp. 39515-39530) announcing that it will be reviewing regulations for the information collection provisions of the Paperwork Reduction Act of 1980.

• October 1982. On October 6, 1982, the Office of Management and Budget released a list of more than 2000 government publications—one out of every six—targeted for termination or consolidation into other publications. This, together with 4500 other cost reductions proposed for an additional 2300 publications, is expected to produce cost savings "of more than one-third." According to OMB 82-25, Reform '88: Elimination, Consolidation and Cost Reduction of Government Publications, "16% of all government publications will be discontinued." This amounts to 70 million copies, 1/12 of the 850 million copies printed, and is part of ". . . the Reagan Administration's continuing drive to eliminate costly, redundant and superfluous publications. . ." Each federal agency will be reviewing its publications for increased user fees.

• February 1983. Public Printer Danford Sawyer presented GPO's budget request for FY 1984 to the House Legislative Branch Appropriations Subcommittee. Of the total FY 1984 request of $129,846,000, $25,738,000 is designated for Superintendent of Documents' programs. The FY 1983 funding for SuDocs was $27,291,000. Reportedly, $900,000 of this cut for the programs of the Superintendent of Documents is to be directed to the depository library program.

Selected Bibliography

Adams, Scott. "Army Medical Library and Other Medical Libraries of the Nation." *College and Research Libraries* 9:126-132.

Advisory Commission on Intergovernmental Relations. *Federal Involvement in Libraries.* Washington, DC: Advisory Commission on Intergovernmental Relations, 1980.

The ALA Yearbook 1981. Chicago: American Library Association, 1981.

Alternatives for Financing the Public Library: A Study Prepared for the National Commission on Libraries and Information Science. Washington, DC: Government Printing Office, 1974.

American Library Association, Washington Office. *Library Services and Construction Act* (pamphlet). Washington, DC: American Library Association, 1979.

Applied Management Sciences, Inc. *An Evaluation of Title I of the Library Services and Construction Act.* Final report prepared for Office of Program Evaluation, U.S. Department of Education, January, 1981.

Avram, H.D. and S.E. McCallum. " Directions in Library Networking." *Journal of the American Society for Information Science* 31:438-444 (November 1980).

Becker, Carl L. "Freedom of Speech and Press." In *Readings in American Democracy,* edited by Gerald Stourzh, Ralph Lerner and H.C. Harlan. New York: Oxford University Press, 1966.

Becker, Joseph, ed. *Proceedings of The Conference on Interlibrary Communications and Information Networks.* Chicago: American Library Association, 1971.

Belair, Robert R. "Information Privacy." In *Issues in Information Policy.* Washington, DC: U.S. Department of Commerce, 1981.

Berelson, Bernard. *The Library's Public.* New York: Columbia University Press, 1949.

Bernays, Edward L. "The Library Inquiry Is Not Over." *Wilson Library Bulletin* 25:245.

Bobinski, George S. *Carnegie Libraries: Their History and Impact on American Public Library Development.* Chicago: American Library Association, 1969.

Boorstin, Daniel J. *The Republic of Technology.* New York: Harper & Row, 1978.

Bostwick, Arthur E. "The Future of Library Work." *ALA Bulletin* 12:51-52.

Bowker Annual of Library and Book Trade Information. New York: Bowker, annual.

Branscomb, Lewis M. "Library Implications of Information Technology." In *An Information Agenda for the 1980s,* edited by Carlton Rochell. Chicago: American Library Association, 1981.

Braunstein, Yale M. "Information as a Commodity: Public Policy Issues and Recent Research." In *Information Services: Economics, Management, and Technology,* edited by Robert E. Mason and John E. Creps, Jr. Boulder, CO: Westview Press, 1981.

Bushkin, Arthur A. and Jane H. Yurow. *The Foundations of United States Information Policy.* A United States government submission to the High-Level Conference on Information, Computer, and Communications Policy. Washington, DC: U.S. Department of Commerce, 1980.

Carnegie Council on Policy Studies in Higher Education. *The Federal Role in Postsecondary Education: Unfinished Business, 1975-1980.* San Francisco: Jossey-Bass, 1975.

Chodos, Laura B., Lucille Thomas and Gladys Ann Wells, compilers. *Third Annual Report From the States, 1982 White House Conference on Library and Information Services Follow-up Inquiry.* Unpublished document presented at follow-up meeting of White House Conference on Library and Information Services Task Force. Atlanta, GA, September 24-26, 1982.

Cohn, John M. "The Impact of the Library Services and Construction Act on Library Development in New York State: A Study in Assessing the Effects of Federal Grants-in-Aid Legislation on the States." Ph.D. dissertation, New York University, 1974.

Cuadra Associates, Inc. *A Library and Information Science Research Agenda for the 1980s.* Final report of a project conducted for the U.S. Department of Education, Office of Libraries and Learning Technologies. Santa Monica, CA: Cuadra Associates, Inc., 1982.

Consumer Media Expenditures 1982-87. White Plains, NY: Knowledge Industry Publications, Inc., 1983.

de Tocqueville, Alexis. *Democracy in America.* Edited by J.P. Mayer. Garden City, NY: Doubleday & Company, Inc., 1969.

Dahl, Robert A. *A Preface to Democratic Theory.* Chicago: University of Chicago Press, 1956.

Data Base/Electronic Publishing Review and Forecast. White Plains, NY: Knowledge Industry Publications, Inc., 1983.

Ditzion, Sidney H. *Arsenals of a Democratic Culture: A Social History of the American Public Library Movement in New England and the Middle Atlantic States From 1850 to 1900.* Chicago: American Library Association, 1947.

Drake, Miriam A. "The Economics of Library Networks." In *Networks for Networkers,* edited by Barbara Evans Markuson and Blanche Woolls. New York: Neal-Schuman Publishers, 1980.

Evaluation of the Effectiveness of Federal Funding of Public Libraries. Study prepared for the National Commission on Libraries and Information Science. Washington, DC: Government Printing Office, 1976.

The Federalist. Edited by Edward Mead Earle. New York: Random House, n.d.

Fry, Bernard M. *Government Publications: Their Role in the National Program for Library and Information Services.* Washington, DC: National Commission on Libraries and Information Science, 1978.

Fry, James W. "LSA and LSCA, 1956-1973: A Legislative History." *Library Trends* (July 1975).

FY 80 Abstracts. Washington, DC: U.S. Department of Education, Office of Libraries and Learning Technologies, 1980.

The Gallup Organization. *Book Reading and Library Usage.* Princeton: Gallup, 1978.

The Gallup Organization. *The Role of Libraries in America.* Princeton: Gallup, 1975.

Garreau, Oliver. *The Public Library in the Political Process.* New York: Columbia University Press, 1949.

Gell, Marilyn Killebrew. "The Ministry of Truth." *Library Journal* 106:399 (February 15, 1981).

Getz, Malcolm. *An Economic View of Public Libraries.* Cambridge, MA: National Bureau of Economic Research, 1979.

Goodrum, Charles A. *The Library of Congress.* New York: Praeger, 1974.

Harris, Louis & Associates and Dr. Alan F. Westin. *The Dimensions of Privacy: A National Opinion Research Survey of Attitudes Toward Privacy.* Stevens Point, WI: Sentry Insurance, 1979.

Harris, Michael H. *The Role of the Public Library in American Life: A Speculative Essay.* University of Illinois Graduate School of Library Science, Occasional Paper No. 117, January, 1975.

Hatfield, Mark. "Library of Congress." *Statesman* (Salem, OR), January 4, 1981.

Havlich, Robert J. "Federal Assistance to Special Libraries." In "Federal Library Legislation, Programs, and Services," edited by Henry Drennan. *ALA Bulletin* (February 1966).

Information for the 1980s: The Final Report of the White House Conference on Library and Information Services, 1979. Washington, DC: Government Printing Office, 1980.

Jewett, Charles C. *Notices of Public Libraries in the United States of America.* Washington, DC: Smithsonian Institution, 1851.

Joeckel, Carleton B. "Questions of a Political Scientist." *ALA Bulletin* 27:66-69.

King, Donald W. "Scientific and Technical Information: Current Issues Concerning Government and this Essential National Resource." Discussion paper prepared for presentation to the Commerce Technical Advisory Board, January 6, 1981.

Ladd, Boyd. *National Inventory of Library Needs, 1975.* Washington, DC: National Commission on Libraries and Information Science, 1977.

Leigh, Robert D. *The Public Library in the United States.* New York: Columbia University Press, 1950.

Markuson, Barbara Evans and Blanche Woolls, eds. *Networks for Networkers.* New York: Neal-Schuman Publishers, 1980.

Martin, Susan K. *Library Networks, 1981-1982.* White Plains, NY: Knowledge Industry Publications, Inc., 1981.

Mason, Marilyn Gell. *Public Library Finance.* Commissioned paper prepared for the U.S. Department of Education, Library Research and Demonstration Branch, November, 1981.

Mason, Robert M. and John E. Creps, Jr., eds. *Information Services: Economics, Management, and Technology.* Boulder, CO: Westview Press, 1981.

Matthews, Joseph R. and Joan Frye Williams. "Bibliographic Utilities: Progress and Problems." *Library Technology Reports* 18:609-653 (November-December 1982).

Mehnert, Robert B. "National Library of Medicine." In *The Bowker Annual of Library and Trade Information,* edited by Filomena Simora. New York: Bowker, 1980.

Meise, Norman R. *Conceptual Design of an Automated National Library System.* Metuchen, NJ: Scarecrow Press, 1969.

Molz, Redmond Kathleen. *Federal Policy and Library Support.* Cambridge, MA: MIT Press, 1976.

"National Agricultural Library Overhaul Urged by Blue Ribbon Federal Panel." *Library Journal* 108:536 (March 15, 1983).

National Referral Center. *Directory of Federally Supported Information Analysis Centers.* Washington, DC: National Technical Information Service, 1974.

Peyton, David Y. "The Creation of Information: Property Rights and Subsidies." In *Issues in Information Policy.* Washington, DC: U.S. Department of Commerce, 1981.

Prentice, Ann E. *Public Library Finance.* Chicago: American Library Association, 1977.

Prentice, Ann E. "Strategies for Survival: Library Financial Management Today." *Library Journal, Special Report No. 7.* New York: Bowker, 1979.

Public Library Association's Coordinating Committee on Revision of Public Library Standards. *Public Library Service: A Guide to Evaluation, with Minimum Standards.* Chicago: American Library Association, 1956.

Putnam, Herbert. "What May Be Done for Libraries by the Nation." Library Journal 26:10-11 (January 1901).

Report of the Trustees of the Public Library of the City of Boston, July, 1852. In Jesse Shera. *Foundations of the Public Library: The Origins of the Public Library Movement in New England, 1629-1855.* Chicago: University of Chicago Press, 1949.

Resnikoff, Howard. *Program Report: Information Science and Technology.* Washington, DC: National Science Foundation, 1979.

Robertson, Lawrence S. and Robert F. Aldrich. "Dissemination of Information." In *Issues in Information Policy.* Washington, DC: U.S. Department of Commerce, 1981.

Robinson, Barbara M. "Cooperation and Competition among Library Networks." *Journal of the American Society for Information Science* 31:413-425 (November 1980).

Rochell, Carlton C. *An Information Agenda for the 1980s, Proceedings of a Colloquium June 17-18, 1980.* Chicago: American Library Association, 1981.

Roosevelt, Franklin D. "To Promote the General Welfare." In *Readings in American Democracy,* edited by Gerald Stourzh, Ralph Lerner and H.C. Harlan. New York: Oxford University Press, 1966.

Science Indicators 1978. Report of the National Science Board. Washington, DC: National Science Board/National Science Foundation, 1979.

Shera, Jesse H. *Foundations of the Public Library: The Origins of the Public Library Movement in New England, 1629-1855.* Chicago: University of Chicago Press, 1949.

Shubert, Joseph F. "The Impact of the Federal Library Services and Construction Act." *Library Trends* (July 1975).

Spivack, Jane F., ed. *Careers in Information.* White Plains, NY: Knowledge Industry Publications, Inc., 1982.

Statistical Abstract of the United States. Washington, DC: Government Printing Office, 1981.

Stevens, Norman D. "Library Networks and Resource Sharing in the United States: An Historical and Philosophical Overview." *Journal of the American Society for Information Science* 31:405-413 (November 1980).

Stone, Elizabeth W. *Historical Approach to American Library Development: A Chronological Chart.* University of Illinois Graduate School of Library Science, Occasional Paper No. 83, May, 1967.

Thomison, Dennis. *A History of the American Library Association: 1876-1972.* Chicago: American Library Association, 1978.

United States Government Manual 1980-1981. Washington, DC: Office of the Federal Register, 1980.

Urban Libraries Council (pamphlet). Chicago: Urban Libraries Council, 1981.

Vagtborg, Harold. *Research and American Industrial Development.* New York: Pergamon Press, 1976.

Warner, Edward S., et al. *Information Needs of Urban Residents.* Washington, DC: Office of Education, U.S. Department of Health, Education and Welfare, 1973.

Yurow, Jane H., Aaron B. Wildavsky and Stanley Pogrow. "Managing Information." In *Issues in Information Policy.* Washington, DC: U.S. Department of Commerce, 1981.

Index

ABOUT THE AUTHOR

Marilyn Gell Mason is director of the Atlanta Public Library. Previously, she served as director of the White House Conference on Library and Information Services, and as executive vice president of Metrics Research Corporation, an Atlanta-based consulting firm. Ms. Mason has also held positions with King Research, Inc.; the Metropolitan Washington Council of Governments; the Arlington County Virginia Department of Libraries; and the New Jersey State Library. A former "Washington Update" columnist for *Library Journal,* she has written numerous articles on the social and political implications of libraries and information policy.